More Than Pretty

More Than Pretty

Doing the Soul Work that Uncovers Your True Beauty

ERICA CAMPBELL

with Beth Jusino

HOWARD BOOKS
—
ATRIA
New York • London • Toronto • Sydney • New Delhi

HOWARD
B O O K S

ATRIA

An Imprint of Simon & Schuster, Inc.
1230 Avenue of the Americas
New York, NY 10020

First Howard Books/Atria Books hardcover edition September 2019

HOWARD BOOKS / **ATRIA** BOOKS and colophon are trademarks
of Simon & Schuster, Inc.

For information about special discounts for bulk purchases,
please contact Simon & Schuster Special Sales at 1-866-506-1949
or business@simonandschuster.com.

The Simon & Schuster Speakers Bureau can bring authors to your live event.
For more information or to book an event, contact the Simon & Schuster
Speakers Bureau at 1-866-248-3049 or visit our website at www.simonspeakers.com.

Interior design by Dana Sloan

Manufactured in the United States of America

1   3   5   7   9   10   8   6   4   2

Library of Congress Cataloging-in-Publication Data is available.

ISBN 978-1-5011-8866-4
ISBN 978-1-5011-8868-8 (ebook)

For my grandmothers,
Ruth Daniels and LeVada Cruthird.
And for all the little girls in the world who
question their beauty, inside and out. May this
book encourage and uplift you.

Contents

I am more than my eyes, my beauty, and my stride
I am built by my trials
I am defined by my confidence and my strength,
my love for life and respect for others
I am defined by my powerful smile
God is my creator and my source
His design is perfect and therefore I am perfected
daily in Christ
For I can do all things through Christ who strengthens me
Yes, I am so much more than pretty
I am working toward being better, stronger, and wiser
I'm becoming a better sister, friend, mother,
daughter, and woman
God's love leads and guides me
It causes me to shine from the inside out
I am so much more than pretty
I am a reflection of God's love for me to the whole world

Love suffers long and is kind; love does not envy;
love does not parade itself, is not puffed up; does not
behave rudely, does not seek its own, is not provoked,
thinks no evil; does not rejoice in iniquity, but
rejoices in the truth; bears all things, believes all things,
hopes all things, endures all things.

—1 CORINTHIANS 13:4–7

More Than Pretty

Chapter 1

More Than Pretty

I'm sitting in the car, waiting to pick up my kids and trying to get a decent selfie for Instagram. So far I've taken at least thirty-seven pictures, and none of them are right. My nose is at the wrong angle in that one. There's a big vein down the center of my head over there. My smile looks stale. Are those wrinkles on my neck? My wig looks too wiggy.

Delete. Delete. Delete.

I take one more. Use a different filter. Okay, that's cute. I can post it.

When we get home, before I even start dinner, I check my page to see how people are responding to the new picture.

"Too cute!"

"lol"

"Looking good!"

And then there it is:

"You're so pretty."

That word has followed me my whole life.

When I was a little girl, people in our church would say "what

1

a pretty voice" when I got on stage to sing. I was a quiet, shy kid in the middle of a big, noisy family of seven sisters, one brother, and two cousins who lived with us because my mom and dad had big hearts. Finding my place was always a challenge, and at home, I spent a lot of time trying to blend in. In church, though, I stood out. I thrived on the love and attention I got when I sang for Jesus. I liked being the girl with the pretty voice, and how people all said I was special.

At the same time, I didn't like being stuck inside for choir rehearsals, especially on sunny Saturday afternoons. And as I got older, I wanted people to see me as a whole person, more than just a voice. I wanted to feel like my pastor and my church family cared about me. There were times I would walk up to the pulpit to sing and God would bless people through my song, but I'd feel miserable. I would be broken but nobody noticed, and that hurt most of all.

By then, it was more than my voice that was called pretty. My mom and my aunt Theresa, the first lady of our church, were always reminding me to "look pretty." Don't leave the house without earrings and lip gloss. Don't wear those raggedy clothes in public. You don't want people to think you're a "bad" girl.

When I was a young adult, single and touring the country as a backup singer for a well-known R&B star, I had a crush on two particular R&B singers who were in the show. In one city, we all happened to be staying in the same hotel, and one night I encountered them in the elevator. As soon as the doors slid closed, we all started laughing and talking, and then they started telling each other how pretty they thought I was. They were using "pretty" to get my attention so they could just casually ask me to "stop by" their rooms.

(By the way, I didn't take them up on their offers. I knew right away that their sweet words were a trap, trying to lure me away from God's plan for my life. Those guys may have said I was pretty, but what they were asking for was a whole different kind of sexy. And no sir, I was not falling for it!)

I went on to sing with my sister Tina as the duo Mary Mary. We won a shelf full of big awards, hit the Billboard charts, and toured the world. We starred in our own reality TV show for six seasons. Then, after almost twenty years of doing music together, Tina and I decided to take some time apart. I'll tell you more about that later. After a lot of work and a lot of prayer, I released my first solo song, which I called "A Little More Jesus." It was a big step for me, and I was proud of the music. As soon as it was out, I went to iTunes to check the reviews. The first one I saw said, "No, honey, you don't need a little more Jesus; you need a little more Tina. What are you doing by yourself? You're the pretty one, but she's the singer."

Okay, that stung really bad. Yes, there have been some doors that opened in part because of how I look, but the reason I stay and the reason my songs continue to reach so many people around the world is because I go above and beyond. I can sing. I've spent years practicing and developing my talent, and I work hard. That song that the reviewer dissed went on to be nominated for a Grammy Award, and it wasn't because of the way I looked.

So yeah, you can say that my relationship with the word *pretty* has been complicated. As a public figure, I'm constantly being judged by how I look and how I act. Being pretty, in some ways, is a job requirement. Yet over the years the pressure of "pretty" has sometimes been a box that felt too tight around me, limiting how I saw myself, how other people still see me, and the places where I could grow. Sometimes it was used to try to manipulate me, bait masked as a compliment.

As I travel the world and talk to women of all ages and backgrounds, I've discovered I'm not alone in this. The pressure to be pretty affects all of us, regardless of our race, our age, our faith, or our family. I've never met a woman who doesn't have her own series of stories about how her desire to be pretty, and the efforts that she's put into it, has marked her life.

So let me say right up front, before we go further: there's nothing wrong with wanting to be pretty. God created us with natural, human desires to be accepted, loved, and appreciated, and the world has always told women that being pretty is the way to get there.

It starts early. If you grew up with a loving or supportive family around you, I bet that when you were a baby, people were happy to see you. Your family smiled when you came toddling into the room, and every time your parents took you out to the store or to church, someone said, "Oh, what a pretty girl." You heard those words before you even remember them, and the message came through loud and clear: people like you and pay attention to you if you're pretty.

Of course, not everyone grew up with that kind of attention. Maybe your family was too caught up in their own issues to fill you with praise, or even to notice you. But there were plenty of other places where society's priorities showed up. You watched movies and noticed that the pretty girls were always rescued from their troubles by handsome princes, but the not-so-pretty sisters went home defeated and alone. At school, you saw how the pretty girls were treated. Teachers paid more attention. Cute guys asked them out. They seemed so happy. And you started to believe that pretty people had easier, better, happier lives.

And of course, how could you miss the whole industry ready and waiting to sell you ways to be prettier?

Centuries before we were using the filters on our phones to make our eyes bigger and our skin clearer, women were buying dyes and powders to smooth their skin and bring color to their lips. Today, your mailbox and your in-box are full of promises to look better, be better, live healthier, and have better sex and a better social life. I've read that Americans spend a staggering $84 billion every year on the creams and dyes and lotions that promise to shrink this and plump up that and cover up something over there, and the average woman in America will spend more than $225,000 on her appearance over the course of her lifetime.

And when it comes to women's efforts to look good on the outside, I'm right there with my credit card in hand. I'm a weird mix of tough city girl and girly-girl, and though I try to be frugal, I love new clothes. Tina likes to tease, saying that "Erica's always gonna have some lashes and lip gloss on just to go have break-fast." That's not exactly true, but I do like to look cute, even when I'm just wearing sweats and tennis shoes to be on the radio at three in the morning, California time. It's important to me that I look like something.

Okay, Erica, that's fine for you. But I'm not into all that makeup and jewelry stuff. I don't take a bunch of pictures of myself. I don't like how I look. Yeah, I hear you. Later in the book, we'll talk more about how God wants us to think about our physical selves, but the short answer is that God gave us our bodies, created us in His own image. God delights in His creation, and invites us to delight in each other. Can you imagine how He must feel, then, when we belittle ourselves or come out with a long list of all the things we think are wrong with us? I think it pleases Him when I make an effort to celebrate and respect what He gave me, and it disappoints Him when I compare myself to others. But I'm getting ahead of myself.

The pressure to be pretty is not just about whether you put on your face every morning or have a closet full of wigs. Women—especially Christian women—are also being pressured to have pretty lives. We think that in order to fit in, we need a rich husband and well-behaved, good-looking kids, a nice house, a new car, and some type of personal business or brand. We need to wear makeup and have gorgeous hair every time we leave the house, and always be nicely styled, poised, and polite. "Living pretty" means living with "good girl syndrome," where we feel guilty if we don't show up at work every day and at church on

Sunday with a smile pasted on and a cheerful voice that assures everyone that we're "just fine, thank you," no matter what's going on. We've got to sing in the choir and cook for the potluck and volunteer at the school because that's just what people expect.

We live with these bogus rules: Don't let the outside image crack. Don't rock the boat. Don't say the wrong thing. And social media has just made it all worse, because we start comparing our insides to other people's outsides—or actually, what we _think_ we know about other people's outsides based on an incomplete picture of what we see from a distance.

From where I'm sitting as I write this, I can see my car parked outside by the curb. From here, it looks all shiny and nice, with a good paint job and tinted windows. Nothing looks broken.

What I can't see from here is that the inside needs to be vacuumed. When I took the kids to school this morning, I saw all kinds of juice boxes and toys and junk in there. And I can't see just by looking at the car whether it's due for an oil change or running out of gas, but if I don't check those things every now and then, I'm risking a major breakdown on the highway.

That's what it's like to only look at the outside of life. You're walking into an enormous house and admiring the nice furniture, not knowing that there are termites in the walls or that the whole foundation is shifting underneath you.

Have you ever run into an acquaintance at the mall and pasted on a bright smile even though not five minutes before you were crying in the car? "Well hey, sis! Yes, all is well, and I'm doing great today." Or have you posted a picture on social media that was the exact opposite of how you were looking and feeling?

Not long ago I was scrolling through Instagram, the way I do, and I saw a friend of mine smiling over brunch with a bunch of her girlfriends. Just a couple of minutes later, she texted me and told me how depressed she was feeling. The pretty image she was putting out to the world wasn't anything like what was happening in her heart.

We've all got to learn to be honest, first with ourselves, then with God.

Life gets out of balance when all we see is what we look like on the outside. If your biggest goal right now is to look good, or your biggest pain is that you don't like the way you look, be careful. Your focus on being pretty has gone too far.

I'm not going to say that social media is bad, because I use it just as much as you do. I love that with just a few clicks on my phone, I can connect and share little corners of life with people I don't get to see very often. I love that when we all get together in person it's like a reunion, because we've seen the pictures and videos and posts about each other's major life events. It's easy to get carried away and to mistake followers for true friends. It's easy to get addicted to the constant feedback of strangers. *People like me!*

But girl, you are so much more than your best filtered photo.

Those images on a screen aren't the real you, and those little hearts and thumbs-up aren't a validation of who you are. No amount of likes or fancy filtered selfies will make you happy.

It's easy to lose sight of that sometimes, because there's a billion-dollar beauty industry trying to convince you that you are nothing more than what you see in the mirror. They want you to buy their cosmetics, use their ad-supported filters, and buy their clothes, so they'll shove professionally photoshopped photos of celebrities on the red carpet in front of you to convince you that you'd be happy if you could only look like this and live pretty like that.

That "red carpet" promise? It's a lie. I've been on dozens of red carpets, and I can tell you that there's just as much disappointment and unfulfilled desire there as anywhere else. People spend thousands of dollars to look their best, but the hair and makeup and gowns don't make them feel loved. A person can win awards and still be sad. Those glamorous dresses are sometimes covering broken hearts and empty wallets. I know, because I've been that person.

Let me tell you what the red carpet at a big award show is really like. You start weeks, if not months, before the event, hiring stylists to find you just the right clothes, shoes, accessories, and (for women with curves like mine) the right undergarments. On the day of the event, you spend hours on your hair and makeup, and then pay people to follow you down the red carpet to "dab" you if you sweat.

You've spent thousands of dollars to be pretty for one night, but even then, the question remains: Are you pretty enough? You can't answer yet. You still have to spend thousands of dollars more to fly your publicist in from New York so that she can walk ahead of you, getting photographers to take the right pictures and asking reporters to interview you. This is where you really have to be made of steel and be very confident, because there will always be people who say no. They're waiting for Justin Timberlake. Or if you do get an interview, the camera that's aimed at you might suddenly shift, and the reporter could walk away while you're in mid-sentence, because Cardi B or some huge actor or actress just arrived.

Once you finally get inside, there's a lot of waiting around while other people have their pictures taken. Everyone's hungry and stressed and giving each other the side eye, because someone has what you want, or wants what you have.

I don't want to sound like it's all terrible. My husband, Warryn, and I have a lot of fun at award shows, and we're blessed to have plenty of friends in show business who help us pass the time. But making appearances like this is part of our jobs, and it's a lot of work and a lot of pressure. What looks glamorous on the outside is also what humbles me and brings me back to Him, over and over.

I've been blessed throughout my life to have a loving family and a successful career doing what I love and what God wants me to do, but it's taken a long time for me to work through the issues that came up throughout my life related to being pretty. It's only recently that I've really understood how those early messages were tests of my spirit, trying to dissolve my identity and thwart my purpose before God could truly use me.

It would be easy, given my line of work, to only think about the things that people see, or to lose myself in the "lights, camera, action." After all, I hire people whose whole job is to talk to me about my image, my photographs, my brand, and my platform. But this isn't unique to show business.

We all like people telling us we're great and people calling our names. It feels good to our egos, but what God's shown me, over and over, is that the surface is just the beginning.

Pretty fades. Pretty changes. Pretty doesn't heal your heart.

Trying to be good enough, cute enough, sexy enough, or nice enough is never going to work.

How do I know? Because I've lived it.

I've stood at the grocery store with a cart full of food for my family and a prayer that my card wouldn't be declined. I've squeezed myself into pants that don't fit as well as they did last week, and I've tucked myself into Spanx so tight I had to sit funny to make sure the seams didn't pop. I've let people see me looking not so cute, with a wig cap on and my hair braided down. I've lost my temper with my family. I've gritted my teeth and pasted on a smile when all I wanted to do was cry over a broken relationship.

In other words, my life probably looks a lot like yours. I've struggled with my body image, focused on my flaws, worried about being truly seen, struggled with being myself, and spent a lot of time trying to understand who I am in God's eyes.

And it's taken me some time and a lot of prayer to come to understand that I'm not just pretty, but also beautiful. He's called me to serve Him with what's inside as well as out—just like He does with you.

In the chapters that follow, I'll share that journey with you.

We're going to talk about that desire to be pretty, and how it plays itself out in our everyday lives. We're going to get honest about our bodies and our sexuality. I'm going to show you the traps that can block you from the future God wants for you, and how to uncover the truly beautiful, richly blessed woman God sees in you. Most important, I'm going to show you how to do the deep, lasting soul work that will lead you to a fulfilling life as a royal, loved, and worthy child of God.

It's not going to be easy, but it will change your life.

Being pretty is where the conversation starts, because we're all on a quest to be more comfortable in our own skin. But this book is about so much more than what we see in the mirror. The conversation needs to grow from there. Who are we as flawed, loved, and hopeful creations? Why are we here? Where do we fit? How can we take the unique strengths that God gave us and use them to best serve Him? How can we own our stories, love our bodies no matter the shape or size, and celebrate ourselves? These are the questions that excite me these days. These are the messages I want to share with you.

This is a conversation that's so real to me, and so present in my life. It comes from the conversations I have every day with my sisters and daughters and cousins and aunts and girlfriends. It comes from the honesty and vulnerability that's been shared at my church's women's ministry, which we named More Than Pretty. We dig deep there, and we get real about mental health and forgiveness and family and relationships. And that's what I want for you, too.

There's a reason you picked up this book. I believe in divine assignments and appointments. Over and over, I've seen God bring me the right people at the right time, sometimes in the most unexpected places. And maybe, for you, this book is that unexpected place. You could be reading anything right now. You could be doing a lot of other things. But something brought you here.

God is leading me to write something now that you're going to need sometime later, wherever you live. I believe that there's something in here that will bless you, change you, shift you, lift you, and help bring you to the next level.

There's absolutely nothing wrong with being pretty, but there's so much more to you than what's on the surface. God has so much more for you.

I'm so excited to share this journey with you.

Chapter 2

You Are Worthy

I want you to know:

You are more than pretty.

You are more than how sexy you are, or how much money you have, or where you live. You are more than what anyone sees on the outside.

You are beautiful, inside and out.

You are created to live a beautiful life.

You are a unique woman with a body, a heart, a mind, and a soul, all created by a God who loves you and finds you worthy of every blessing. You are beautiful because He made you a person worth celebrating. You have a purpose for being on this earth, which is to live fully as a reflection of Him.

Beauty is that inner core of who you are, created by God and molded by experience. It's not just the shell of what people see, but the sum of your thoughts, your dreams, and your desires. Beauty shines from the inside past the surface.

I love the way beauty is described in the NIV translation of 1 Peter 3:3–4, "Your beauty should not come from outward adornment such as elaborate hairstyles and the wearing of gold jewelry or fine clothes. Rather it should be that of your inner self. The unfading beauty of a gentle and quiet spirit, which is of great worth in God's sight."

Being "pretty" is all about what you look like on the surface, but living in beauty is deeper and more robust. It comes from your soul and reveals itself through your confidence and compassion: how you carry yourself, how you take care of yourself, how you speak to people, and how you show your love and care for the world around you.

To live in your fullest beauty, you have to dig deep and look with open eyes at every part of yourself, even the ugly stuff. True beauty comes from vulnerable honesty; there's nothing cute about a lie. Pretty hits the surface of nice, pleasant Erica, but who I really am, and how I really live, depends on what's underneath—the beauty that's at your core.

For some of you, this is an almost impossible thing to wrap your head around. You have a tough time seeing the beauty in yourself. Your core feels damaged. For years, maybe your whole life, you've felt like nothing more than a body, and a faulty one at that. People ignored, ridiculed, abused, lied, betrayed, or abandoned you, and maybe your own choices in response weren't good. Now it's difficult to see yourself as anything other than damaged goods.

If that's your story, then this chapter is for you. Later, we're going to dive deep into the ways that you can live more fully in your beauty and grow toward your purpose, but before you can take on that level of soul work, you need to be able to look honestly at the things you've been trying to hide, to bring them to God, and to still see yourself as worthy of His investment.

I promise, whatever you've got tucked away in your closet, you are still worthy.

Even if your past is a mess, you are worthy.

Even if no one before has ever told you how important you are to God and to the world around you, you are worthy. God has called me here to tell you that. As busy as I am with my husband and three kids, a church, two music careers, a radio show, and a TV show, I had to write a book for you because I truly love people. Even if I've never met you in person, I know you are beautiful and you are loved because you are a child of God. You are unique and special. If we do ever meet, I will give you a hug and tell you face-to-face.

But maybe not even that will be enough. Maybe there's some story weighing down your heart that's holding you back from even starting the journey, or asking the questions, that will lead you to the place where you can see yourself as God sees you. There's something that makes you think you're less than the other people around you. Before we can go forward with this book—before we can start the soul work that will help you grow into the strong, deep, beautiful woman God made you to be— we need to identify those things and bring them into the light.

For some women, their messy pasts make them think they're not beautiful. Trust me, I know what it's like to live through stuff.

I know what it's like to have to overcome hardship. My story has its share of dark corners. The smile that I wear and the confidence that I have are not because I've never experienced anything bad. I'm not going to tell you about anything that I didn't have to live first.

Here's the thing to remember, though: we always have a choice in how we see our circumstances, and in how we live. The bad things that happen, and the negative things that we hear, don't have to control how we live, or even how we see ourselves. They don't have to keep you from becoming everything God wants you to be. Let me give you some examples.

Yes, I grew up in a Bible-reading, Jesus-loving family. My parents loved us. My dad was a preacher with a gift to minister to people on the streets, and my mom was a preacher, too, as well as the church's piano player and choir director. But when I was a kid, we were "economically challenged." Okay, basically, we were poor. There's no other word for it. We were a family of ten, and my dad had a lot of health issues, and he and my mom had a difficult marriage. They actually divorced and remarried each other three times while I was growing up. My family was on welfare for a few years, and we moved around a lot, usually not by our own choice. I remember coming home after school one day to find a huge truck parked in the front yard and all of our things in bags outside. My mom was there, telling me to grab as much stuff as I could because we needed to go live with Grandma or an aunt again for a while.

I could have grown up believing that I would always be poor and let that limit my dreams and choices, but I didn't.

I remember being a little girl, upset at having to move again, and thinking, *You guys are always talking about what God can do, but clearly He's not getting our calls and prayers, because we keep getting put out.* When we did have a house, the roof leaked. Kids at school made fun of me for wearing the same clothes all the time. Sure, I would go to church and have a good time, but I still had to come home to reality.

I could have become bitter at God, believing that He had failed us, or that it was His obligation to give me what I wanted right when I thought I wanted it, but I didn't.

Like most teenage girls, I had my share of boyfriends who broke my heart by not calling often enough or having another girl on the side.

I could have believed that all men were dogs and buried my heart behind a wall so thick that no one could ever get past it, but I didn't.

I watched my grandma live in constant pain after an accident, and my dad suffer with an undiagnosed adrenal illness that kept him on medication his whole life.

I could have lived in fear, believing that my body, too, would break, but I didn't.

When Tina and I moved out together into our first apartment, sometimes I didn't know how we would pay our rent. We constantly prayed that our cars would keep running. I had to shop at the 99 Cents store for everything from towels to groceries.

I could have believed that we were never going to be able to support ourselves and given up my dream of a career in music before it even started, but I didn't.

Then there was the painful year when I found myself standing on stage, singing "take the shackles off my feet" and "I can't give up now" every night, even as I was having major problems in my marriage.

I could have believed that my only option was to walk away, giving in to pain and never forgiving or seeing my husband through God's eyes, but I didn't.

My circumstances have never been perfect, but I've come through. Over and over, there have been situations that tried to trip me up, that could have led me to give up before I even got started. God always protected me from letting my challenges and trials change my beliefs.

God has a plan and a purpose for you that's bigger than your circumstances, but you have to be ready to let go of any bitterness, or fear, or jealousy, or anger about the things in your situation that don't seem fair. Whatever happens, you can choose to trust that God is good, and that He loves you and is creating a destiny for you, even when things don't go according to your plan.

There are a lot of people who want you to believe that if you serve God and love God, everything in your life will work out right. If you pray and go to church, you'll get the husband and the house and the full bank account. Well, that's not true. God is not a genie in a bottle, waiting to give people whatever they want just because they show up. "In the world you will have tribulation," Jesus told the disciples in John 16:33. The more successfully you serve God, the more it will seem like turbulence is popping up in your life.

Yet God's power guides us and guards us even in the hard times. As I look back, I can see how He used those challenges of my early life to prepare me for the blessings He set aside for my future. Those hard things I talked about before didn't prevent me from being worthy of my destiny; they made me tough enough to handle everything that came later, and He can do the same for you. There is always hope!

God's Word is full of stories of women whose faith was tested by some serious stuff. Sarah's husband, Abraham, put her honor and dignity at risk when he lied about their relationship to protect himself from men who lusted for her. Ruth became both a young widow and a refugee, following her mother-in-law to a strange country with strange customs, so poor she had to live off the charity and food scraps of others. Esther was married to a controlling husband who abused his first wife. These are not the parts of their stories we usually tell—we like to jump ahead to the victorious parts—but before the victory come the struggles.

Every day, you can choose to walk in the footsteps of those Bible heroes, trusting that no matter what things look like in the moment, God has a plan, and He will bring the victory. Your job is to trust your future to Him. Even though I've been sick, I always knew God was my healer, and I didn't have to stay sick. Even though I've had my heart broken, I never believed that my heart had to stay broken. I made the choice to trust God, and through Him, to trust people. I smiled even if there was a tear in my eye, because I believe that God has a plan and a purpose for me, and that these trials and tests are only here to make me stronger.

I would never be where I am today if I hadn't looked past the reality of my situation, time after time, to stand in faith and believe that God had something better for me. I believed the dreams that God allowed me to dream and accepted the possibility of who God showed me I could be.

He has the same promises for you.

I don't know your story. I don't know if you've lived with divorce, abuse, financial hardship, grief, addiction, or something just as painful. What I do know is that whatever happened, it doesn't change the way God sees you. It doesn't make you less precious to Him, or limit the future He has for you. Your past is the past, and it brought you to this place, right where God wants you to be.

Here's the other thing about your past: it also doesn't excuse you from the responsibility to take care of yourself, inside and out, and to live a life worthy of your calling. You, too, need to be tough enough to take the blows and keep living.

Like I said, life is life. You will feel uncomfortable at times, and you will go through things that hurt. But when you realize that the ultimate outcome of every single thing that happens is the opportunity to bring more glory to God, your spirit can be lighter because the victory is already yours.

So if you are tempted to feel paralyzed and stopped by the pain of your past, I challenge you to believe the report of the Lord and what He says about you. Reject the criticism of other people. Reject the voice in your head that tells you nothing will change.

Whatever your story is, God can step in and transform it if you let Him. Nothing in God's kingdom is wasted. Nothing that you've been through will be wasted. You'll find your true beauty, as well as your true calling, when you open yourself to embracing His future, no matter what was in the past.

But Erica, you don't understand. You don't know what I did, how bad I messed up. There's no way to get past that.

It's one thing, after all, to get hung up on the things we can't control. It's something else to get past the things that we've actually done ourselves.

If you're a woman who has spent more than a little time in this world, chances are you've done some things that you're not proud of. Mistakes were made. Maybe they were big mistakes, things that left scars on other people. So now you may feel like wherever you are and whatever your life is like, you deserve it. *This is what I get. This is the consequence of my actions.*

When you screw up, the voice in your head whispers that you're a fraud because you say you believe one thing but act another way. It tries to convince you that the truth isn't just "I did something wrong." It wants you to believe that "I *am* something wrong."

I'm here to tell you that no, you're not. You may have made a mistake, but you are not a mistake. There's nothing that the love, the mercy, and the grace of God can't cover—no issue, no care, no concern, no sin, nothing. Jesus knew what you did before you did. He knew it even before He went to the cross for you.

Just look at the Bible: most of the heroes there are former

murderers, adulterers, liars, hypocrites, thieves, and worse. Yet God used them, just as He will use you. He will always use a life that is totally surrendered to Him.

When I was a young, single woman, I made some mistakes that left me feeling like everyone around me was talking about me. The details don't matter here—it was nothing sinful, but it was really public. I felt like everyone in my church, especially, knew what happened. I dramatically told my mom I was going to New York to stay with an aunt and uncle so that I didn't have to face anyone.

"Don't do that," my mom said. "Just come back with your head up. You can live anything down. There's nothing God's grace and the cross don't cover." And she was right. When I released my own shame and condemnation, and stopped worrying about how much people knew, I could move forward and live. I had to forgive myself. I had to repent, change, and surrender it to God.

If we're going to step forward in the following chapters to explore how to live the full lives that God desires for us, we need to receive all of His grace and all of His mercy. Romans 8:1 says, "There is therefore now no condemnation to those who are in Christ Jesus." If God has set you free, be free.

Whatever area of brokenness surrounds you, you are not a broken person. You are forgiven. All you have to do is ask, according to 1 John 1:9: "If we confess our sins, He is faithful and just to forgive us our sins and to cleanse us from all unrighteousness." Leave those tears in yesterday, and embrace the new you.

It's time to stop looking backward, and start looking to a future that's in line with God's plan. If you did go the wrong way at some point, separating yourself from God's will, there's always an exit ramp from the road you've chosen. There's always a way out. There's always a way through. There's always a way over. You can always come back, and God will be just as merciful and loving with you as He has always been, and as He is with anyone else.

What's true about your past is also true for your present. Once you set off on this journey toward living your beauty, you're still going to make mistakes, and you're still going to feel like everything's going sideways. But you always, always have a choice.

There are days I'm not home when one of my kids wants me to be there, and times I give a concert when my energy just isn't there. There are times I'm totally present and on top of things as a wife, or the feeling on the stage is just powerful and anointed. But then, other times, I'm sick or distracted or just plain tired. My ability doesn't always meet everyone's expectations at every moment.

I used to let those "off" days get to me. I felt the weight of my responsibility to my family, to my staff, and to my fans. I would stand on a concert stage and look out at people I knew had planned months ago to come there, who had traveled and had sacrificed to buy their tickets. I would stand in the doorways of my children's rooms and watch as they slept, wondering what they would remember about growing up with a mom like me. I want to give them all as much as I can, as much as I have, but sometimes that still isn't enough.

Just a few days ago, I had one of those moments. I'd been

working long hours, flying back and forth across the country, jumping from one meeting to another, all *go go go*. That's how it usually is for me, sixteen hours a day, and most of the time, I'm okay with it. But that day, I hit my end quick and fast. One minute I was present and engaged, and the next I was just *done*. I was empty. I couldn't talk to one more person or shake one more hand.

I should have prayed for patience and strength to complete my assignment. Instead, I headed for the door. "Lord," I prayed, "let me get out of this room, because I'm going to be rude in about 2.2 seconds." I knew that "Nice Erica" had already left the building, and so I just got up and followed her to the car while my team was still working.

I could beat myself up over that, just as I could beat myself up over any of the dozens of mistakes I've made. But you know what? God understood me in that moment. He offered me grace, and so did the people around me. He knew how tired I was. They understood that I wasn't trying to be a diva or disrespectful.

We've all been there, haven't we? The responsibilities we shoulder make us feel far from God's grace. Your daily schedule might not look like mine, but I'm certain there are things that make it feel all but impossible to make time to think about being a child of God, let alone try to live like one.

Sometimes, those moments of darkness, which come from the world's false messages about how we should look and how we should act and how bad we've screwed up, are loud. I get that. I've done my time there.

For six seasons, my sister Tina and I not only sang together, but we also shared our lives in a reality TV show called *Mary Mary*. Those were some tough years for us both, and the cameras were right there to capture the good and the bad in our families, our ministry, and especially our relationship with each other.

There was one time I remember in particular during the last season when I just broke down in front of the cameras. It was not pretty. Even though we were a few hours away from a huge and important performance, there was no glam and no glitz in my life. I was crying all over the place.

For a lot of our viewers, it was a surprise to see me like that. Usually, I'm the cheerful one. My outlook on the world is so optimistic and hopeful that Warryn once called me "Alice in Wonderland." But real life can be hard, and even the most positive people like me can get caught up in it. That night, I was just plain Erica, empty and in need of God's direction. I was overwhelmed and hurt. Everything seemed unfair. It felt like I was working for God, but He wasn't working for me.

At times like that, I don't feel like doing the soul work. I don't want to hear the Word of God or sing another gospel song. And when things are hard, let me tell you, I *definitely* don't want someone to come along and tell me "you're going to be all right, because God loves you."

Yet in those times, that's exactly the message I need to hear the most. And if you're in a place that feels hopeless right now, it's what you need to hear, too.

Are you spiritually stuck, distracted, feeling out of sorts or empty? God loves you. Are you looking at your life and struggling to find hope for the future? God loves you. Is it hard to look in a mirror and see your value as a child of God? God loves you.

We all reach points and times where we feel empty. I don't care if you're a professional entertainer, you work in a corporate setting, or you're in full-time ministry. Sooner or later, life will make you feel like you are nothing, that life is nothing, and that all you have is failure. But that is not God's truth, and it does not have to be your truth.

The Bible says that "the trying of your faith worketh patience." Sometimes our minds wander and circumstances get hard, and we get discouraged. That's okay. It's a human reaction. The important thing is to not get stuck there. God brings the dark times to build our endurance and to help us see ourselves, and to understand Him, in new ways.

What you're having is a low moment, not a low life. You might have broken times, but you're not a broken person.

If you find yourself getting stuck, be honest about how you're feeling in the moment. Give yourself time for some healing tears if you need them, and then assess where you are and take the necessary steps to pull yourself out of that place. You can't do it on your own, so rely on supernatural intervention. Open your Bible. Pray. Call your pastor or spiritual mentor.

In our lowest moments, the best thing we can do is tap into something greater than ourselves.

When things are hard and I'm starting to doubt myself,

I love to think about the breadth and complexity of creation. God made whales, alligators, and zebras. He made living things of every size and every need. And He did it all intentionally, in ways that balance the world. He did it all in the right order; He didn't make the fish and then the water, because He knew what the fish needed. He created a prepared and pH-balanced ocean first, and then the animals went in.

And if He could make all of that work out so well, then surely He has your plan figured out, too.

On those days when I'm empty and someone else is reaching out and needs more, I'll go as far as I can—that's my responsibility—and then leave it up to Him to fill the gap. When I've had three hours of sleep, and my child is sick, and I need to be on an airplane the next morning, all I can do is turn to God and ask Him to bring the ends together.

When I was crying in front of those cameras, at the end of my rope and maybe my career, I heard God whisper that I am stronger than I think I am, and promise that there's purpose in my life. He still had an incredible destiny for me. I remembered the verse in 2 Timothy that says, "For God hath not given us the spirit of fear, but of power, and of love, and of a sound mind."

In that moment, I knew I would be okay. And so will you.

Whatever has happened, whatever you've done, whatever darkness you've walked through, God is still there. He's ready and waiting for you, but the choice is yours.

Almost twenty years ago, Warryn suggested that we name our singing duo Mary Mary. At the time, Tina and I had no idea how much it would grow, or how often we'd have to explain that name. (No, my name is not Mary, and neither is my sister's.) But God did. He knew where He was taking us, and so He gave us a name with a message.

See, Mary Mary is named after two of the most famous women in the Bible. The first was Mary, the mother of Jesus, who was faithful and pure her whole life. The other is Mary Magdalene, who was, well, not so perfect. The Bible says she was filled with evil spirits but she was delivered, and she was one of the first to see Jesus after His resurrection.

Two women, with two different stories, who were both vital parts of Jesus' ministry on earth, and both changed by the power of His love. A person's past doesn't limit how God can use him or her.

I love the Scripture in Psalm 34:5 that says, "They looked to Him and were radiant, and their faces were not ashamed."

It's time to get rid of those shadows of shame. It's time to bring your doubts, your hurts, and your mistakes into the light so that they don't have power over you anymore. Nothing you've done in your life disqualifies you from experiencing the love of Jesus, and His love can change anything in your story.

So if there's something weighing you down, or sitting between you and God, write it down. Don't just type it on your phone. Find a pen and a piece of real paper. Get honest. *Okay, this happened.* Then write down your release. *It shouldn't have, and now it's over. I've repented, I've turned away from it. It's over* now, *and it's not hurting me anymore. I'm not worried, I'm not bur-dened, because Jesus is love and His grace has covered this issue.*

When you're done, burn that paper. Turn it into ashes, and as you watch it disappear, watch your past mistake disappear with it.

It's time to put aside the negativity. It's time to stop holding on to the past and release the guilt and the fear. It's time to embrace our power and our femininity God's way. It's time to move forward to live lives that are more than pretty.

As Warryn and I tell our kids all the time, *Don't get scared. Get ready.*

When I think about moving forward and living as a beloved child of God, I often think about the games my siblings and I played outside when we were kids. Hide and Go Seek; Mother, May I; Red Light, Green Light; Tag—there were lots of different games, but they all had one thing in common: base. If you got to the base, you were safe.

I think about those games now when I read Proverbs 18:10: "The name of the Lord is a strong tower; the righteous run to it and are safe."

God provides us with a "base" in life, a safe place where we can go when things are tough. But sometimes people get carried away with doing their own thing, and they venture too far away from the base, just like we did when we were kids. They live in places that are not safe.

If you want to move past living on the surface, the first step is to get back to that safe place, the base, where you can see the world through God's eyes. The journey there is the process I call soul work.

"All things are possible to him who believes," Jesus says in Mark 9:23. But until we know what to believe, we don't have a place to start. God made you beautiful, and there is a destiny for you, but it doesn't fall in your lap.

If you want to live deeper than the surface, you need to do the work to develop your spiritual IQ, your ability to hear God's voice.

Just as your body needs attention in order to be healthy, so does your mind and your spirit. You can't fill yourself with nothing but junk food and expect your muscles to support you for long. You need to commit to the things that nourish you and build you up. Paul describes it to the Philippians when he says, "whatever things are true, whatever things are noble, whatever things are just, whatever things are pure, whatever things are lovely, whatever things are of good report, if there is any virtue and if there is anything praiseworthy—meditate on these things."

Living in God's fullness and purpose, as beautiful women, comes from spending time with Him in His Word, in worship, in prayer, in church, and in communion with our Creator. The more time you spend listening, the more you will hear clearly. The more you follow His voice, the more His plans seep into your soul and guide your decisions. His desires become your desires, and His plans become your plans.

Did you catch that? When you live in God's purpose, on purpose, you make the decision to completely submit yourself to His plan.

A lot of times, it's not easy. In the past few years, God has called me to some really uncomfortable places. He has shifted me into becoming a solo artist, a radio show host, and (most surprising of all, at least to me) the first lady of a growing church. Every step required me to dig deep and gather my spiritual IQ, my confidence, and my knowledge of God and myself. But every step of the way, God was right there beside me to remind me that He'd already put everything inside me that I needed to become everything He wanted me to be.

When you're in tune with God and living in faith, He will show you a new way to live, one that will leave you blessed and beautiful. He will assure you, over and over, that you, too, have everything inside you that you need to become everything that He wants you to be.

The rest of this book is here to help you explore that deeper life. We're going to talk about the things you can do to discover the beauty that God has put inside you. We're going to dive deep into the Word of God, because that's where all truth comes from, but I'm also going to ask you to look at your daily life. We're going to talk about the words you use, the friends you keep, and even the way you treat your body.

I need to warn you, this isn't a book you can just read and put aside. You're going to need to think about what's here. You're going to need to find your own path to the place where you feel confident with yourself and with God's plan for you. I'm going to lay out the things I've learned, as well as a lot of my pitfalls and questions, but your story is not my story, and your path is not my path. The things I share and tell may not be a perfect fit for where God is leading you. So start each chapter with a heavy dose of prayer, and end it with an honest evaluation of how the words apply to your life.

Take your time, because you are worth it. You are beautiful.

Chapter 3

Deceived and Distracted

"She's probably having sex."

I was just sixteen years old, minding my own business and making my way toward the door at the end of church one Sunday, when I saw two ushers looking at me. The older usher said those words just as I walked by.

I acted like I didn't hear her and kept walking, but I was crushed. I was a church girl, raised in a family of believers, and I was the kind of person who did everything I could to make my parents proud and Jesus happy. I knew plenty of girls my age who were sexually active, but I wasn't one of them. Yes, I had curves, but not going too far with a boy was one of the most important rules of being a good girl, and I wanted with all my heart to be a good girl.

So why would the usher say something like that about me? Was I giving off some kind of bad vibe? Was I wearing something that gave people the wrong idea? Was I walking a certain way? Was I too confident, smiling too much, too happy? That usher's words wounded my young heart, and I started to question everything about my appearance, the way I carried myself, and how God and other people saw me. A seed of doubt was planted that day that stayed with me for years, making me always conscious of how I expressed myself as a woman and what other people saw in me.

Looking back, I can see how that day in church was another test, an attempt to break my confidence and do permanent damage so I couldn't see myself through God's eyes.

For as long as women have been taught that our appearance matters, our bodies have been used against us.

In my colorful imagination, there's a conference room in hell, and in that conference room is a whiteboard with your name on it. And on that whiteboard, the enemy—call him Satan, the Devil, Beelzebub, Evil, whatever you want—and everyone who works for him keeps track of your weak points, your temptations, and the places where your heart has been broken in the past. I imagine them talking about me the day that I overheard the usher. *Let's attack her self-esteem now. She's got a big assignment in her life, but if we catch her now at sixteen, if we jab at her now, by the time she is in ministry, she'll be too damaged to fully live there.* These are the things that can keep you from achieving everything that you're capable of doing. The enemy will use the issues of life to make you envious, jealous, doubtful, and fearful, and, he hopes, eventually convince you to give up.

In his quest to keep you from God's full blessing, he will not limit himself to the truth about your life, either. The enemy is the ultimate deceiver. In John 8:44, Jesus calls him "a liar and the father of it." He's been lying since the beginning of time, when he went to Eve in the Garden of Eden and told her that she should eat from the Tree of Knowledge. He flattered her, tempted her, and lied to her until she looked away and began to question what God said. That changed the whole of human history.

Today he uses those same lies to deceive you, distract you, and separate you from the blessings God has for you. He will do everything he can to worm his way into your life to damage your reputation and make you look crazy. The more you grow in your walk with Christ, and the more influence you have in the world, the more he'll take your image and your words and twist them to trick you.

In fact, the base of the word *pretty*, in English, comes from an old Germanic word, *prat*, which as recently as the fifteenth century meant tricky, cunning, and clever. In other words, being "pretty" used to mean being a trick or a distraction. It pointed to the smoke and mirrors of an attractive face.

How much of that is still accurate today? How much does the enemy still trick us into holding ourselves back and drawing the wrong kind of attention to ourselves, all because of some mixed-up idea we have about being pretty by someone else's standards?

Make no mistake: our enemy has no new tricks. He can't force you to do anything. He can't take your hands or control your feet to make you do something you don't want to do. But he has thousands of years of practice with lying, and he will tell you anything he can to knock you down. He will whisper in your ear 24/7, pointing to the things you see online or on television, or at the people you know who seem to have it better than you. He will use everything around you to make you think that you're *less than*, *not enough*, or *damaged goods*.

Every woman I know, from the youngest to the oldest, has wrestled with questions about how the world sees her outsides.

After I grew up and got married, I became the auntie whom a lot of my nieces and cousins came to for advice, especially advice about boys. When we were kids, my sisters and I all went to our aunt Theresa's house when something happened. If you broke up with a boyfriend, or you got scared about something, you went to Aunt Theresa's. Well, now my house is becoming that safe place for the young women in the family.

I love having this role, and I'm completely honored, but man, sometimes the questions are hard. "Am I a nasty girl?" they ask me, because they, too, grew up in church and knew "the rules" about not going too far with a boy. They aren't sure how to hold onto that standard when there are boys who want to kiss them . . . and even more confusing, boys they want to kiss.

As my own daughters have grown, the questions and challenges have gotten closer to home. My oldest, Krista, was fourteen when I started to sense that something was bothering her at school more than she was letting on. We were in the middle of taping a season of our family's reality TV show, *We're the Camp-*

bells, and so the cameras were on when Krista and I sat down to talk. I thought that she was going to tell me about her friends at school, maybe about a boy she liked. Instead, Krista got deep and real.

She told me about how she felt left out, "on the side," because she was chubby and, in her words, "the fat friend." She told me that boys also weren't interested in her because they like light-skinned girls and she's darker than her friends.

That's not what I was expecting at all, although I guess I shouldn't be surprised by her eloquence and understanding. Krista has always been articulate and poised beyond her years. At three years old, she would walk up to strangers in elevators and introduce herself: "Hi, my name is Krista, and this is my friend Mommy." So sure, it makes sense that she would be healthy enough at fourteen to give voice to the issues of colorism that so many African-American women today carry. But I wasn't sure I was ready to have those conversations with my daughter, my baby. That's a tough one for any mom.

There have been plenty of off-camera conversations with Krista since that one, and I'm still working on how to handle it well, in a way that will help my daughter understand how beautiful she is. She continues to be inspiring in her honesty as she talks to Warryn and me about her struggles to accept her skin and her weight. She envies her cousin Eniyah, who is very slim. But when I talk to Eniyah's mom, she tells me how her daughter wishes she had curves like Krista.

And all I can think about, when I look at them both, is a song

that Tina and I wrote and recorded as Mary Mary way back in 2002,
long before Krista and Eniyah were even born, called "Little Girl."

She was just thirteen and I just don't think
That she'd ever seen her own beauty
She didn't think she'd be anything
And little girl, she used to be me

Little girl, little girl
Wonder are you listening
Little girl, little girl
Struggling with your confidence
Little girl, little girl
God made you so beautiful
Little girl, little girl
I just thought that you should know

Sometimes you feel like you don't fit in
'Cause you don't look like all your other friends
You got your own thing going on
Girl, you're so unique. You are just
The way that God intended for you to be

Tell you what you should do when you get up in the morning
Look yourself in the mirror and say I love me
Even with all your flaws and all of your downfalls
Just be your best 'cause to Him you already are.

When I wrote that song, I was remembering my own awkward years, and all of the complicated feelings that went with not knowing yet who I was. Tina and I weren't mothers ourselves yet, but we were surrounded by sisters and nieces and cousins who were trying to find themselves in a messy and confusing world. Now, there's a whole new generation of thirteen-year-olds who've got their own thing going on. And every single one of them is beautiful.

The enemy has us distracted, and we're all tied up in knots over this issue of pretty. No matter what we look like, or how old we are, or where we live, or how much money is in our wallets, we can get stuck in the lies. He's confused us—tricked us, to use that old German word—into tangling up God's perspective of who we are with the world's ideas of pretty and sexy. He's led us into temptation by bringing us people who are full of manipulative praise and attention when we're feeling empty, and then he uses those people to take us away from who God wants us to be.

Single women tell me they long to be married and wonder why they're not attractive enough to find the right man. Married women email me about how they wish they had more time to take care of themselves. Older women talk about how, as their sexual presence fades into menopause, no one seems to notice them at all. Women of all ages who've had their hearts broken in love tell me about their feelings of failure and rejection.

We all long to be seen. As we move and grow from one season to the next, we all struggle with knowing how to live. It's not always easy to believe that we're good enough to be loved and honored for who we really are when the enemy has tied our ideas about our outside appearances into something much deeper and more dangerous: low self-esteem.

This is a thing I talk about so often that I shorten low self-esteem to LSE, an acronym I got from my *Get Up! Mornings with Erica Campbell* radio show cohost, Griff. He uses it to describe the times we write ourselves off before we even begin. When someone comes in the room and says, "Hey, I know you guys are really busy and you don't really have time for me . . ." Griff will pipe up, "LSE!"

Low self-esteem is the feeling that you are not as good, or not as worthy, as someone else. It's the voice of the critic inside your head that says people won't like what you have to say before you ever open your mouth. It's the reason you believe that everyone will judge and reject you because of your size or your skin or your clothes or what's in your wallet. It's the voice in your head that is constantly comparing you to others and saying that you don't measure up, killing every ounce of motivation in your body.

LSE is what makes you respond to compliments with deflection. You can recognize it if you start every conversation with an apology or preface what you say with an assumption that the other person isn't going to listen. LSE makes your posture bad, because something inside you wants to physically tuck and cover with shame, or shrink to a place where you're invisible.

LSE whispers that someone didn't call you back because they think something terrible about you, when really they probably just got busy with their own stuff.

Low self-esteem makes you pay more attention to what other people might think about you than about what you think of yourself, or even what God thinks of you. You create these ideas that other people all have perfect lives—that they're always pretty—and that you're the only one who's trying to cover up and filter over the messy stuff. It leaves you constantly in fear of judgment. *Will they like me? Will what I offer be enough? What will that fine man I'm interested in think if he sees my flaws? What will happen if I don't say the right thing, or if that family comes to my house and my table's not set... or if I don't even have the money to own a table? What will the women at church say if my kids get in trouble or have the wrong kind of friends?*

I'm just as guilty of this as anyone, no matter how positive I try to be. Someone says, "Your skin looks great!" and I respond, "Girl, I had to exfoliate this morning because I had bumps everywhere." Or "Oh my gosh, you look so good," and I wave it off with "Girl, that's because I've got this body shaper on." The older I get, the more I'm aware of this bad habit, and I try to catch myself. I have to remind myself to just accept the compliment and say "thank you" without diminishing myself or the person who's being kind to me. The world will dish out enough abuse; I don't need to add it to myself. But it's definitely a learning process.

There was a time in my career when I would stand on the sidelines at the big award shows, festivals, and gatherings. I was already in Mary Mary, selling albums and winning awards, but I still felt intimidated. Everyone else seemed more beautiful, more successful, more famous, more anointed. My low self-esteem ate at me, and if it had grown, it could have sabotaged what God was doing through me. It could have caused me to waste time, doubt my calling, and minimize my position.

But then, one day, as I walked away from yet another gathering, I heard the Holy Spirit tell me loud and clear, "I've given you everything you need to be everything that you need."

In that moment, I realized that I already carried the anointing of God. I carried the power of God. I carried His love, His peace, and His grace inside of me. What else could I possibly want?

From then on, my confidence grew as I learned to rely not on what others thought of me, but on who God made me to be. Now when I walk into a room, I don't care who's there, because I know that I'm necessary, I have something valuable to add, and I'm enough. I understand that I'm living in my purpose and on purpose, by God's design. There is nothing missing and nothing lacking. What else could I hope for?

The enemy loves to use LSE to make us doubt ourselves, even to hate ourselves. We don't call it self-hatred, of course, because that sounds bad. But when we minimize ourselves and diminish ourselves, that's what it looks like and feels like.

But Paul says in Ephesians 5:29–30, "For no one ever hated his own flesh, but nourishes and cherishes it, just as the Lord does the church. For we are members of His body, of His flesh and of His bones." We are God's creation, and we are made for His glory. He made us with glory inside of us so that we can reflect that glory back to Him. How can we feel bad about something that is created with a little piece of God's glory?

That doesn't mean it's always easy to remember that, though. Not long ago, I led a mirror exercise for the women's ministry group at my church, the California Worship Center. I brought each woman a beautiful little hand mirror and asked her to hold it. And then at one point, I asked them all to look at themselves in their mirrors and tell their reflections that they are beautiful.

I didn't realize when we started how hard it would be for them. For the next few minutes, some of these women I've come to love like family—women of all ages, sizes, races, education levels, and backgrounds; women who are married, single, divorced, and separated—hesitated. They mumbled, and they laughed nervously. Some of them grabbed their mouths, as if to hide the words. As I watched, I was struck by how much they didn't want to say it.

These women, every one of them beloved by God, were uncomfortable with acknowledging their own beauty as His creations.

The enemy will always give you a reason not to feel good enough, always put something and someone in front of you to compare yourself to. There's always some failure to remember and magnify as if it just happened yesterday. But none of that matters, because God deems you worthy: worthy of love, worthy of success, worthy of peace, and worthy of acceptance.

Why? Plain and simple, because He loves you. Going back to Ephesians, this time chapter 2:4–8, with my emphasis added:

*But God, who is rich in mercy, **because of His great love with which He loved us,** even when we were dead in trespasses, made us alive together with Christ (by grace you have been saved), and raised us up together, and made us sit together in the heavenly places in Christ Jesus, that in the ages to come He might show the exceeding riches of His grace in His kindness toward us in Christ Jesus. For by grace you have been saved through faith, and that **not of yourselves; it is the gift of God.***

Jesus went to the cross for every single issue that you have ever dealt with. For every indiscretion or sin, the blood of Jesus covers you just as much as it covers the person next door. Jesus loves you more than you could possibly imagine.

The enemy doesn't want us to see the glory that we are granted simply because we are God's creation. He does everything He can, and always has, to make us not see the beauty of who we are as unique individuals—how much God delights in how we look, how we talk, how we laugh, how we see the world. Instead, he plants the seeds of division and LSE so that we measure ourselves against others and only see our faults and our flaws. "Well, I didn't go to church, and I made this mistake, and I messed up that relationship." He wants us to beat ourselves up. He wants us to doubt ourselves. And most of all, he wants us to doubt God.

But our Heavenly Father doesn't compare us to other people. God doesn't measure us by what size we wear, or how clean our kitchen is, or whether we're doing all the right things on the outside. We're going to look at this more deeply in Chapter 4, but what I want you to know now, here, is that God doesn't judge you by someone else's life.

Not all of the enemy's attacks will be internal whispers of doubt. Sometimes the attacks come straight from the mouths of other people. Someone makes a cutting comment on your social media page, or you overhear people saying something about you that you wish you hadn't. A well-intentioned friend or relative will awkwardly mention that you've gained a few pounds or suggest a diet plan that worked for her. She'll look surprised when you feel hurt.

Because so much of my life is public, sometimes those experiences with other people happen right out there in front of everyone.

For example, there was the white dress.

It was 2013, and I was about to release my first solo album. I'd also just given birth to our third child, Zaya. During the photo shoots for the album's packaging, I posed for a series of pictures wearing a white dress. Well, actually, it was a white top and skirt, but thanks to the magic of photo touch-ups, it came out looking like a dress.

I was totally covered from my neck to my shins, but the outfit clung to my new-mama curves. I felt good when I wore it, and when I saw the final image I thought I looked good—strong and sexy and confident, but still classy. I sent it to Warryn and my family, and everyone loved it.

It was supposed to be my album cover, but my publicist jumped the gun a little and used the image for a press release announcing my Grammy Award nomination for the single "A Little More Jesus," and it just went viral—not the song, but the picture. Overnight, it seemed like everyone had an opinion about what I was wearing, and there was a lot of ridicule and criticism. People all over the country were posting on social media, and a lot of them were accusing me of not being "Christian enough," or of being a bad example for other women. There were plenty of other people who stepped up to defend the picture, too, saying I looked great, and the whole thing became a big debate.

For the next few months, the white dress caught everyone's attention. I made the rounds of media to talk not about my new album, but about how I felt about the body God gave me. At the time, I thought it was the worst thing that could happen. It hurt to hear the negativity. There were pastors saying that I must be trying to draw "the wrong kind of attention" to myself. But why would I do that? I didn't need anyone's "wrong" attention. I was happily married. I already had awards on the walls and a new album ready to come out, and this kind of thing wasn't going to help me sell more gospel music.

I felt like the sixteen-year-old girl in church all over again. *I didn't do anything bad! I promise, you guys, I didn't.*

Looking back, I can see how the whole thing was another attack, trying to break my confidence and make me doubt myself when I was right at the edge of launching into so many important new things. I can also see how the controversy started a conversation in the Christian community that we needed to have. It made people in the church ask themselves what it means for a woman of God to look good, to feel good about herself, and even to look appealing. It made me realize how much believers needed more conversation about body image and self-acceptance and, yes, even sexuality—the beauty and splendor of woman that God created within the body of Christ.

In hindsight, I can even see how that white dress led to this book. It's just another example of how God takes what was meant for evil and uses it for good.

God created us with a need for each other. He filled us with a desire to be loved and accepted. That's not a bad thing. It's what brings us together. But the enemy has taken that need and corrupted it. When people turn against you, it's easy to believe their criticism and feel worthless. When they fill your head with praise, it's easy to start to listen to them more than to God.

He's used our positive desire for connection to distract and deceive us. His tricks have led to millions of toxic relationships—not just romantic ones between men and women, but also toxic friendships, toxic work relationships, and even sometimes toxic churches.

I've met so many artists and musicians who have been swayed by the voices of the crowd. They start to believe their own hype, and they start to rely on their fans' enthusiasm to fuel their passion. Suddenly, it's no longer about singing for Jesus, or even for the music itself. It's all about hearing the praise of other people.

But this is not just a problem for celebrities. In this digital age, we're all exposed to the attention of the crowd. No matter how many "likes" we get, it's never enough. No matter how many people praise us, there will always be someone to test us or make us doubt ourselves all over again. There will always be a critic there to shoot us down.

Your desire for validation can get mixed up with your human need for love. Your sense of self and identity can get confused with the adoration of strangers, but that only touches the surface, so it will never fill the real God-shaped hole inside you.

You don't have to believe the deception. You don't have to be a victim of the enemy's lies or your human tendency to compare yourself to others.

James 4:7 shows you the way. "Therefore submit to God. Resist the devil and he will flee from you."

I love my work, but when I submit myself to God's plan, I know that my needs for love will be met by Him first, and then by my family. The affirmation of others is the icing on the cake. And while I appreciate everybody that has ever supported me in any way, I've come to understand that public attention is fleeting, and there will always be someone new coming up to capture some of the attention.

For twenty-five years, the memory of that usher in church look-ing at me and then telling her friend "she's probably having sex" has stuck with me. It's plagued me. It's changed me. But then, just recently, as I was writing this book, I realized something.

What if she wasn't talking about me?

I never asked that usher about her words. I never asked her what she saw when she looked at me that day, or what she meant when she said "she's probably having sex." I made a lot of assumptions, but now that I look with the benefit of hindsight, I was one person in a crowded church. What if the usher wasn't even looking at me? What if she was talking about someone else? What if I misunderstood the whole situation?

This is how the enemy deceives us. Can you see how I owned the negative words and opinions of people when I didn't need to? At sixteen, the thought of being judged, and being seen as bad, made me feel bad about myself. The whole thing was a setup to make me feel judged and condemned, and I hadn't done anything wrong.

God didn't see me through the eyes of that usher that day. He doesn't see you through the eyes of your ill-wishers today. He has called you to something entirely different, something bigger and better.

There's nothing that's too hard for God to handle. There's nothing that we can't win with His help.

I love that there are so many songs in gospel music about winning, because so often, we're stuck in the thinking that we're losers. We believe that God's perfect plan is there for everyone except us. We believe there's nothing we can do to change our situations, and we're trapped by our circumstances.

But God promises that He'll do "exceedingly abundantly above all that we ask or think, according to the power that works in us." Jesus says that when you work through the power He gives you through prayer, you can change the very atmosphere around you. You can be a winner in every area of your life if you first make up your mind that you're going to let Him lead you to victory, and then do the work through Him to make it happen.

When you work your power, you can be so excellent at your job that your boss can't help but give you that raise and promotion. You can make a difference in your neighborhood. You can even use your power to change the spirit in your house. If you have negative family members or people who are not saved, bring peace to your house through the prayer that Joshua prayed: "As for me and my house, we will serve the Lord."

When you are on the road to victory, other people's opinions cannot stop you. The enemy cannot stop you. Only you can stop you. It's time to turn your attention away from his lies, away from the opinions of others, and back to God.

And that's what we're going to talk about next. When we submit ourselves to God and to who He says we are—when we resist the enemy and let God's definition of beauty cover us—we'll be ready to move forward into a new place. When we let ourselves be transformed by the renewing of our minds, and see ourselves as God sees us, and do the work to develop not just our outsides but also our inner lives, then we'll be in a place to experience the fullness of the life He wants us to have.

Chapter 4

Look in God's Mirror

I spend a lot of time posing for photos, from formal studio shots to silly selfies I take with my kids. There's almost never a day that I'm not recorded somewhere, somehow. But out of all those images, there's one pic that I think is my favorite. It's a candid shot of me that Warryn took the year we got married, and you know what? I was a hottie. I'm laughing on the beach, wearing a bathing suit and looking skinny and happy and full of energy.

To be honest, that picture is everything I wish I could still look like.

At the same time, though, when I look at that shot and remember that day, I think, *Oh, twenty-something Erica, there were so many things you didn't know. You thought you were hot stuff, with your new husband and your music taking off. You had no idea what else was coming. And while I would certainly like to have your body size again, I wouldn't trade my hard-earned wisdom for it.*

That's the thing about pictures: they only show us what's on the surface. If you dig into your phone or your social media and look at a recent shot of yourself, you'll probably see what the world sees at first: the shape of your face, the color of your eyes, the style of your hair, the way your clothes fit. You may also see signs of how you felt at that moment—how tired you look because you're working hard to keep everything afloat, or the extra sparkle in your eyes because there's a fine man standing there beside you. You might notice that you're wearing raggedy old sweats because you've been stuck inside with a new baby for days, or a cute dress because you're enjoying a night out with your girls.

Yeah, you'll probably see your flaws and the things that you never like about how you look. But also, take the time to see something that makes you happy. Maybe you can tell that your time at the gym is paying off, or you were having a good hair day.

Your photo tells a story—your story—but its focus is too narrow to capture the whole scene. It doesn't reveal what was happening in your head or in your heart, or what was happening outside the frame. You could have been standing there looking amazing, but two feet away, everything was falling apart.

The same is true when you try to see your inner self through the lens of your own human perspective. When you stand in front of your mirror or in front of other people, your ego focuses on the surface. Do you look right? Are you acting right? How do you compare? But by now you know that what you look like on the outside isn't the whole picture.

Let's look at the ways you can start to see yourself through God's mirror to reveal what He sees in you.

In the last chapter, we talked about low self-esteem, or what I call LSE. That's when you doubt yourself for no good reason. I want to talk about something different here—ego. *Ego* is a fancy word for the way our human minds see how we fit in the world, what we're doing, and how we measure up to what's around us. When I look up *ego* in the dictionary, the synonyms are *self-esteem, self-importance, self-worth, self-respect, self-image,* and *self-confidence.*

Look, there's nothing wrong with confidence. One of the things I want you to find in this book is greater confidence in who you are and who God created you to be. But that kind of confidence—as well as esteem, importance, worth, and respect—is not meant to come from your *self.*

Your *self*-driven ego looks at a situation and says, "I did this." It sees how you just got a few compliments, or a few new social media followers, or a few more dollars in your pocket, and thinks, "I earned this, and it is what I deserve." When things are good, your ego starts feeling like you're something special, maybe even better than someone else.

Your ego draws attention to what *you* think, what *you* see, and what *you* want. You're in the center of the frame, the star of your own show, and there's no room for anyone else. That's why I always say that ego stands for "Easing God Out."

There have been plenty of times when my ego got the better

of me as a musician. Especially in the early years of Mary Mary, I would tell myself, *We wrote that song that everyone loved. We toured. We won the award. I have the knowledge and the talent, so ask me, don't tell me, what to do or how to act.* If a manager or promoter or even a family member would suggest that maybe Tina and I should be doing something different, I would remind them what we had done. Nicely, of course, but my point was clear.

When Mary Mary's manager suggested that we needed to do something different after our second album didn't launch with the same sales as the first, I decided instead that he needed to go. (Side note: most people probably imagine that Tina did our dirty work, because she's more publicly outspoken than I am, but anytime we needed to let an employee or manager go, it was on me.)

To be honest, I didn't talk to God about firing that manager, and I let my ego lead the conversation. I decided that he was against us. My attitude that day was *this guy can't tell us what to do. He can't tell me this record isn't good. We wrote "Shackles." We won a Grammy.*

Later, when I realized I'd handled it wrong, I apologized and mended the relationship, but bringing that kind of ego to my career has led me into plenty of other ditches. I've refused good advice and charged ahead. I've decided that God didn't want anybody to crush my spirit and ignored the Holy Spirit's quiet question, "Are you *sure* that's what you want to do? Have you talked to God about this yet?"

My *self*-confidence and *self*-image were the enemy's tricks to make me think that the pictures I had of myself came from my own efforts. When things were going well, he wanted me to believe that I deserved what was happening, or that it was happening because of me. He wanted me to feel full of myself and entitled, rather than humble and open to direction.

More often than not, when my ego took over, that project failed. I'd get on stage in front of a crowd, and the presence of God would not be there with me. And then, when I was back on my knees asking what happened, I would hear God saying, "You didn't invite me in."

Just so we're clear: these weren't bad things I was trying to do. I was working on songs that praised Jesus and events where we sang to honor Him. Just because something didn't work doesn't mean it wasn't a worthy project. I was doing the right things with the wrong attitude. I was relying on my own ideas and pushed the Creator of the Universe to the sidelines. My ego eased God out and took credit for His success.

Piece by painful piece, I've had to learn to get over myself, to "lean not on my own understanding," as the Bible says, "but in all my ways acknowledge Him." I had to understand that my view was limited, but His was eternal.

Nothing that's happened to me or to Mary Mary was because I was all that special. Tina and I didn't have some divine revelation of how "Shackles" would change the world when we recorded it in a garage, squeezed up against an old VW van. I didn't realize that God's grace would allow that record to sell 500,000 copies. It all happened because of God's perfect picture and plan. My albums and songs and awards are all here only because of Him, and only He sees the full picture of how they can be used. I don't have to understand. I just have to trust Him.

I am a glory reflector, not a glory producer. Whatever I have, God has blessed me with it. I didn't do any of this myself. If I am great, it's because God placed greatness inside of me.

I thank God for His mercy and grace. I thank God that there's always another chance to get it right. Because my enemy wasn't a manager or promoter. My enemy wasn't my sister or whoever I was mad at on a particular day. My enemy was Satan, and he was using my own ego to try to distract me from the ministry that I was there to give.

What happens if you stand in front of a mirror for a few minutes and look at yourself not through your ego, but through God's eyes? Don't shy away. Don't get distracted by the surface. Instead, meet your gaze and hold it there for a moment. Because when God looks at you, He sees the eternal you—the part of you that's real and unchanging. He sees your soul.

Are you wearing an "I don't care" attitude like a wall to block off the world, or are you flashing some kind of false humility? Is there a tilt to your chin that says "don't talk to me, or I might go off"? Or are your shoulders hunched with defeat, and the desire to not be seen? He sees those things. He looks at whether you are working in your gifted areas, serving Him.

When you stand with God, He doesn't judge you by the

shape of your nose or the size of your bank account. He looks at how you're living in community with Him and with others. He looks for your humility, your willingness to turn off your ego and listen. He looks at whether you are patient, kind, and honest with others.

Can you see what God sees in you? Can you step back from your own ego, and your own sense of self, to understand your true, eternal value and worth? When God looks at you, He sees a piece of Himself, because you were created in His image. And helping you see that is the next step in our soul work together.

If you grew up in church, surrounded by believers, sometimes your Christian walk is just the result of going along with the crowd. Your mom believes, your dad believes, and so you believe.

For me, my father, Eddie Atkins, was our family's walking Bible. That man knew every Scripture and how they all connected. Anytime an Atkins needed to understand God's Word or God's will, we'd call my daddy. He would tell us to get out a Bible, and then he'd help us find the right verses. He would give us a breakdown of how everything connected and what it all meant.

But faith isn't a family inheritance that just gets passed down from one person to another. It's got to be inside you, guiding how you think and feel and experience the world. You can't stand on God's truth if you don't know it yourself.

Long before we started Mary Mary, one of my sisters had a

boyfriend who called me out on this. "You don't really know the Bible," he told me one night. "You only know what your pastor says. You don't know God; you only know what your mom and dad say." He was just playing, but his words stung. Was there truth in them? Was I living my life based on something I didn't really know and believe?

I sat down that night and tried to remember all the Bible verses I knew by heart. At first, I got a little freaked out because I could remember a verse here and there, but I didn't know where they were found, I wasn't totally clear on what they meant, and I didn't know much to the letter. I hadn't studied! Was I equipped to be a Christian if I didn't really know the Word?

God, I prayed, *I need more information.*

I pulled out a piece of paper and tried again, deciding I would write down every verse I knew. I started with the basics—*For God so loved the world . . .* and *I can do all things through Christ who strengthens me.* And the more I wrote, the more I remembered. By the time I finished, I had filled a page.

That wasn't a lot, considering how many pages are in the whole Bible, but it was enough for me to realize that yes, I did know God. Maybe I didn't know all of the generations of kings and judges, and I realized I had a lot more to learn, but I knew those verses on my piece of paper were the core of who I was. And now that I knew what I knew I knew, I could build on that core. I committed to learning more Scripture, more promises, and more truth.

I started adding to that piece of paper, trying to memorize

more and take in more Scriptures. As an artist, I started to sing the Scriptures more, and I sought out artists whose songs reflected the Word of God.

My sister's boyfriend is long gone, but the journey he started in me continues. Today, my faith is my own, and it's rooted deep inside me. Nothing can separate me from the love of Jesus.

When my father died, my family went into shock. Even though his children were all grown and had our own relationships with God and, for many of us, our own ministries, he was still our walking Bible. The moment he passed, everybody started asking, *What are we going to do? Who's going to teach us the Word of God? How are we going to learn?*

Even though I'd been studying the Bible for years on my own, it was my father's death that forced me to start really trusting that God would lead me directly. God says that He is "near to those who have a broken heart," and my heart was fully broken. He promises that He will direct my ways, and I wasn't sure where I was going. In my grief, those verses that I'd read so many times came fully to life. Scripture became my Band-Aid and my healing ointment.

When I claimed the promises I knew, He stood by them, and He was there.

Is it possible to see in yourself what God sees?

Absolutely. God is not some mysterious, distant, or unknowable being. If you're a believer, God is inside you and all around you, and He's surrounded you with ways to find the answers you seek. But you have to be intentional about looking for them, thinking about them, and living them.

If you're looking for Jesus, He promises you will find Him. It's that simple.

Jesus tells us in John 14:26 that "the Helper, the Holy Spirit, whom the Father will send in My name, He will teach you all things, and bring to your remembrance all things that I said to you." I love the idea of calling the Holy Spirit a "helper." So often, people write the third part of the Trinity off as just a feeling or something weird or even scary, the thing that gives them goose bumps. But the Holy Spirit is just as real as the Father and the Son. He's the part of God who lives inside us. He is a comforter and a guide, promised by God and freely given to believers.

That quiet voice in your mind that God uses as a compass to point you in a right direction? The little whisper that you might describe as "something's telling me that I should . . ."? That's the Holy Spirit, offering you the best vision of yourself and reflecting to you what He sees of who you can be.

He's always there, if you are listening.

Because I claim what the Bible says, I can stand in front of any mirror, and on any stage, with full confidence of what my true reflection shows:

I am a daughter of God, fully loved and completely reliant on His care and grace. I am a flawed human subject to divine leadership. I am a faint reflection of the righteousness of God, filtered through what Jesus did on the cross.

I'm loved. I'm special. I'm royal. I'm forgiven. I'm unique.

On my own, there's not much that I deserve. Like any other human being, I'm a messy, sinful, flawed creation. But God loved me so much—He loved us all so much—that He did something radical. He offered His own Son as a sacrifice to make up for all of my mistakes, and make me righteous and pure in His eyes. When He sees me, I am pure and flawless.

God looks at my heart, in other words. And that's where my attention needs to be, as well.

Do you believe that? Do you know, without a doubt in your heart, that God sees you personally, knows you personally, and speaks to you personally? Are you confident in His commitment to a relationship with you? Because everything after this relies on that. Your future growth relies on knowing that you can hear from Him when you need Him.

Yeah, okay, Erica, I hear what you're saying. *I want to seek, but HOW? I can't just go to the store and pick up some Bible knowledge along with my chips and salsa. I can't order a monthly subscription to the Holy Spirit. What does all of this look like in real life? Do you have some fancy acronym for me to remember, or have you uncovered some secret path to the Holy Spirit no one's ever experienced before?*

The world is always trying to convince us that we need something new, but that's not what I have for you here. All I can tell you about building your relationship with the Holy Spirit is what has worked in my life and the lives of the people around me—the same thing that Christians have been doing for two thousand years.

"Abide in me," Jesus promised His disciples during the Last Supper, and He will abide in us. That's it. It's so simple and so hard.

Lucky for you, God has given you the tools to find Him.

We know that God is not interested in how the billion-dollar cosmetics industry plumps and smooths and covers your outsides. Instead, He offers what I call "kingdom cosmetics," or the spiritual tools that protect and cover you, and that last longer than any set of eyelashes or cream. Outer cosmetic companies focus on the shell, but the Holy Spirit's kingdom cosmetics accentuate, build up, and protect what's inside you.

Maybe you've heard about these kingdom cosmetics before, under a different name. Paul calls them the "armor of God" in Ephesians 6:13–17:

> *Therefore take up the whole armor of God, that you may be able to withstand in the evil day, and having done all, to stand. Stand therefore, having girded your waist with truth, having put on the breastplate of righteousness, and having shod your feet with the preparation of the gospel of peace; above all, taking the shield of faith with which you will be able to quench all the fiery darts of the wicked one. And take the helmet of salvation, and the sword of the Spirit, which is the word of God.*

If we want to be in tune with the Holy Spirit, and see ourselves through the eternal filter of God's lens, then we need to wear the armor we're given as believers—truth, righteousness, peace, faith, salvation, and prayer. After all, cosmetics don't do any good when they're sitting on a shelf.

Look at your past week. How much time did you spend reading God's Word? Was it the first thing you reached for every day, even before you start scrolling on your phone? Was it the last thing you looked at every night? Don't get intimidated by the size of the Bible or the style of the language. God has given you a brain that's big enough to understand a few "thees" and "thous"—and if not, there are plenty of versions that are written in plain English. If you're not a reader, pick up an audio version of the Bible and listen every day.

Meditate on it and let it come alive. Don't let anything else replace it. I'm a songwriter, so I know that yes, music can be a worship tool to help you grow in your relationship with God, but nothing is as solid as the actual words of Scripture. God never promised to stand by my word. He promises to stand by His Word.

Let the Holy Spirit lead your reading. You don't have to read the whole Bible, cover to cover and front to back. If there are five strong Scriptures that you know beyond a shadow of a doubt, and you can build on those, then that's where God wants you. He might lead you to meditate on one single verse for a month or six months, because He wants to reveal something from each and every word in the text. Go with that. It's more important to linger, pray, and follow the Spirit than it is to speed read a bunch of pages that don't stick in your heart and mind.

As you linger on the Scriptures, read them out loud. Speak

their truth over your life. We'll talk about that a little more at the end of the chapter.

How often do you pray? "Pray without ceasing," the Bible says in 1 Thessalonians. God doesn't just want to hear from you when you want something or you want to complain about something. That's not how healthy relationships work. He wants us to have conversations with Him, sharing the good things as well as the bad. He wants us to stop and say thank you once in a while.

In John 15, in the same conversation where Jesus tells His disciples to abide in Him, He also says that a branch cannot produce fruit if it is severed from the vine. And we cannot be fruitful unless we remain in Him.

Only God's way gets God's results. Whatever tree you are attached to, wherever your roots go, that's what you will produce. If you try to hold onto little bits of yourself—a little envy here, a little jealousy over there, a little hatred toward just that one person—and think you're going to still feel the blessings and comfort of the Holy Spirit, you're going to be unpleasantly surprised. Those things will weaken your connection.

God promises us an abundant, blessed, and overflowing life, but only if we do the work. You have the key, but it's up to you to put it in the door.

So read your Bible. Pray. Plant your roots in a good, Bible-teaching church. Surround yourself with the guidance and encouragement to live right, to always try to know God better.

And then look in that mirror again, and you'll see yourself as God sees you.

Think about it like this: Imagine an artist or a sports team that you really get into. You probably consume as much about them as you can. You watch all of their shows or games and listen to all of their music. You google them. When you meet other fans, you get excited to talk about something you both love.

Now imagine that you've been given an all-access pass to that artist or team. You've got front-row seats, backstage or locker-room passes, entrance to VIP suites, chances to meet the celebrities, everything. But you never go. You never show up at a game or concert, you never meet anybody, you never do anything.

When I ask you why, you say, "I'd have to drive and park and walk and keep track of tickets and things. It's all just too much work."

That's what it's like when you have salvation and you don't make the effort to activate the Holy Spirit in your life. Through salvation, you've been given an all-access pass to the Creator of the Universe, but you have to make the effort to use it.

And don't tell me you don't have time. If I can do it, with three kids and just as many jobs and a crazy travel schedule, I know it's possible. I'm not perfect, and my spiritual growth is still a work in progress. I struggle with procrastination, and I need to regularly pray for God to help me be better, to remember to make more time for Him than I do for Instagram. He has to remind me often that my strength is going to come from time with Him, not time reading the comments.

But the key for me, I've learned, is to infuse God into every moment and to prioritize Him in every open corner of time. God can meet me anywhere. So maybe I don't have a regular Bible hour every morning, but when I need my Jesus time, I make my Jesus time. I know I can't function on my own for too long before I start feeling discombobulated in my heart, and I know it's time to stop and reconnect with the Source.

If I'm on a plane, I open the Bible app on my phone. I listen to worship music while I'm exercising. If I'm at home and I need some Jesus time, then we're going to order pizza instead of Mom cooking dinner tonight. I'll sit in the car outside my house and listen to a devotional message or pray before I bring in the groceries. If I'm sitting in traffic, I'll turn off the radio and say, "Jesus, can we talk?" Or more often, I'll feel Him tug at me and say, "Erica, it's time to talk." And we do.

Those are the moments when God will really reveal Himself to you. He'll change your direction, focus your attention, and remind you that it's all about Him.

Another way to kick-start your soul work is with an exercise of affirmations.

Have you ever spoken affirmations into your life? Those are the words and ideas that you say over and over, usually out loud but sometimes in your heart, until they are ingrained into your mind and your belief.

If this is new to you, bear with me. I believe in the spiritual realm. I believe that the enemy and God are real, and that there are angels surrounding me and protecting me. I believe that words have incredible power. Everything God did, He *spoke* into existence. When Jesus *told* the demons that they had to go, then they had to go.

When we speak the Scriptures out loud, we claim them. There's research that says that if a person hears something often enough, positive or negative, that message becomes part of the person. So if a sister is filled with fear all the time, and she owns those fears, accepting them rather than rejecting them, then the spirit of fear fills her. It goes and sits on her lap, because she's claimed it for herself.

In the same way, when you speak positive, powerful words of blessing and claim them for yourself, believing that they are part of you, then the Holy Spirit fills you, pouring the power of those blessings into your life. The Bible is full of promises about how God will honor and reward those who call on Him and use His name.

So I'm going to challenge you now to do something brave. Before we go on together, stop and fill your mind with what God says He sees when He looks at you. Everything that follows hinges on you knowing these truths about yourself.

After this, I promise that I'll get back to stories about my music and show business life, and about my family, and about how I got here. But God's words are more important than anything I can say to you about myself. So if you can, read these out loud. If you're feeling really brave, do it while standing in front of a mirror. Look at yourself and see the person God promises you are.

This is your true, eternal reflection:

I am the righteousness of God.

God made him who had no sin to be sin for us, so that in him we might become the righteousness of God. (2 Corinthians 5:21)

I am fearfully and wonderfully made.

I praise you because I am fearfully and wonderfully made; your works are wonderful, I know that full well. (Psalm 139:14)

I am a promise and a possibility.

Blessed is she who has believed that the Lord would fulfill his promises to her! (Luke 1:45)

I am worth it.

Indeed, the very hairs of your head are all numbered. Don't be afraid; you are worth more than many sparrows. (Luke 12:7)

I am destined for greatness.

"For I know the plans I have for you," declares the Lord, "plans to prosper you and not to harm you, plans to give you hope and a future." (Jeremiah 29:11)

I am blessed.

But blessed is the one who trusts in the Lord, whose confidence is in him. (Jeremiah 17:7)

Blessed are those who hunger and thirst for righteousness, for they will be filled. (Matthew 5:6)

I am lovable.

For God so loved the world that he gave his one and only Son, that whoever believes in him shall not perish but have eternal life. (John 3:16)

A new command I give you: Love one another. As I have loved you, so you must love one another. (John 13:34)

I am a good friend.

Do not let any unwholesome talk come out of your mouths, but only what is helpful for building others up according to their needs, that it may benefit those who listen. And do not grieve the Holy Spirit of God, with whom you were sealed for the day of redemption. Get rid of all bitterness, rage and anger, brawling and slander, along with every form of malice. Be kind and compassionate to one another, forgiving each other, just as in Christ God forgave you. (Ephesians 4:29–32)

I am fun.

So I commend the enjoyment of life, because there is nothing better for a person under the sun than to eat and drink and be glad. Then joy will accompany them in their toil all the days of the life God has given them under the sun. (Ecclesiastes 8:15)

I am happy.

Rejoice in the Lord always. I will say it again: Rejoice! (Philippians 4:4)

I am forgiven.

If we confess our sins, he is faithful and just and will forgive us our sins and purify us from all unrighteousness. (1 John 1:9)

Be kind and compassionate to one another, forgiving each other, just as in Christ God forgave you. (Ephesians 4:32)

I am a sister.

Do nothing out of selfish ambition or vain conceit. Rather, in humility value others above yourselves, not looking to your own interests but each of you to the interests of the others. (Philippians 2:3–4)

I am a daughter.

"I will be a Father to you, and you will be my sons and daughters," says the Lord Almighty. (2 Corinthians 6:18)

I am covered.

He will cover you with his feathers, and under his wings you will find refuge; his faithfulness will be your shield and rampart. (Psalm 91:4)

I am strong.

The Lord is my strength and my shield; my heart trusts in

him, and he helps me. My heart leaps for joy, and with my song I praise him. The Lord is the strength of his people, a fortress of salvation for his anointed one. (Psalm 28:7–8)

I am powerful.

But he said to me, "My grace is sufficient for you, for my power is made perfect in weakness." Therefore I will boast all the more gladly about my weaknesses, so that Christ's power may rest on me. (2 Corinthians 12:9)

I am a worshipper.

Praise the Lord, my soul; all my inmost being, praise his holy name. (Psalm 103:1)

I am a prayer warrior.

I urge, then, first of all, that petitions, prayers, intercession and thanksgiving be made for all people—for kings and all those in authority, that we may live peaceful and quiet lives in all godliness and holiness. This is good, and pleases God our Savior, who wants all people to be saved and to come to a knowledge of the truth. (1 Timothy 2:1–4)

I am a giver.

Each of you should give what you have decided in your heart to give, not reluctantly or under compulsion, for God loves a cheerful giver. (2 Corinthians 9:7)

It is more blessed to give than to receive. (Acts 20:35)

I am patient.

Be completely humble and gentle; be patient, bearing with one another in love. (Ephesians 4:2)

Be still before the Lord and wait patiently for him; do not fret when people succeed in their ways, when they carry out their wicked schemes. (Psalm 37:7)

I am kind.

Those who are kind benefit themselves, but the cruel bring ruin on themselves. (Proverbs 11:17)

I am trusting.

Trust in the Lord with all your heart and lean not on your own understanding; in all your ways submit to him, and he will make your paths straight. (Proverbs 3:5–6)

I am compassionate.

Therefore, as God's chosen people, holy and dearly loved, clothe yourselves with compassion, kindness, humility, gentleness and patience. (Colossians 3:12)

The Lord is compassionate and gracious, slow to anger, abounding in love. (Psalm 103:8)

I am more than pretty.

Charm is deceptive, and beauty is fleeting; but a woman who fears the Lord is to be praised. (Proverbs 31:30)

I am beautiful.

Your beauty should not come from outward adornment, such as elaborate hairstyles and the wearing of gold jewelry or fine clothes. Rather, it should be that of your inner self, the unfading beauty of a gentle and quiet spirit, which is of great worth in God's sight. (1 Peter 3:3–4)

(All verses in the above section from the NIV.)

Do you feel it, how the Holy Spirit weaves through those verses and into your heart? This is what happens when you claim Him.

God—the Creator of all life and matter, the architect of our universe, the savior of humanity, the all-knowing, all-perfect Father of us all—loves you. You, specifically and personally. He knows your name, your story, and your thoughts. He is committed to you so much more than you know, because you are someone who should be loved.

He has equipped you for the life He's given you, and He has big plans for you.

What will tomorrow bring? Only God knows. What we know is that His word tells us one thing over and over: God has a purpose for every one of us. He made you with so much potential inside you. There are so many blessings waiting to fall into your lap, and so many opportunities for you to share your hard-earned knowledge and experience with this world.

So the next time you look at a photo or in the mirror, look for that person who is full of potential greatness. See yourself as God sees you.

Chapter 5

Know Yourself

By the time I was twenty-one, I had been engaged to be married twice. I know, I know—by today's standards that's young, but I was a girl who loved love. I remember thinking I was in love with the boy who pushed me on the merry-go-round when I was in kindergarten.

The first guy I said I'd marry was such a mistake that I don't even need to tell that story, but the second guy was a super-handsome chocolate church guy. He lived halfway across the country, but our families had been friends for years, and we all visited each other a lot. He was cool and funny and romantic. One time, he FedExed me a package filled with rose petals and a handwritten love note. He paid attention to me and filled me with compliments. He was the life of the party every time he came to LA.

He loved music and loved God. His dad was a pastor at a church like mine. Our relationship seemed, on the surface, like God's gift. We were going to have the best life ever.

I started to plan for a move to a place where it snowed, and we set a wedding date. I reserved the caterer and flowers, and my sisters all gave me deposits for their bridesmaid dresses. My "happily ever after" seemed like it was about to happen. But the closer the wedding got, the more I felt a tug in my spirit that something wasn't right.

Whenever we talked about the future, my fiancé would minimize my music aspirations. I had always been clear with him that the Lord called me to become a singer, ministering to and blessing people. He knew I was actively pursuing singing opportunities in LA. But he didn't seem to get what that meant for us, or for him. He told me that I could sing at his dad's church on Sundays, but he wanted me to have a "real job" during the week. According to him, families were only successful if both husband and wife worked outside the home, and singing wasn't something he considered work.

But wait, I was singing when you met me, and I'm not stopping! That tug on my heart got a lot stronger.

If someone showed up on your doorstep right now and offered you something you'd always dreamed about, would you know if it fit what God wants for you? Do you know yourself like that— not the person people think you are, not who they want you to be, not who you want to be, not even who you hope that someone thinks you are, but who you really, truly are when it's just you and God in the room?

If you want to live a life that's deeper than the surface, filled with God's blessing and joy, you won't get far if you don't know who you are. Joy comes from living in God's purpose on purpose, and that comes from understanding where you fit in His eternal plan.

As a woman, your desire to be pretty is mostly a desire to be seen by others, to be appreciated and loved and blessed. But before anyone else can truly appreciate you, you have to appreciate yourself. Before anyone else can know you, you have to know yourself. There's no one else in the world who can fully understand you like you do.

Knowing yourself is no small project. This will be hard soul work for you. It takes time spent in quiet places, away from your phone and your kids and your work. It takes confidence that those affirmations we read together in the last chapter are true. And it takes your willingness to step out in faith, trusting that God created you with a unique, important purpose that's entirely your own.

No one else can do this for you—this is not a project for you and your girlfriends, or your small group, or even your husband or your pastor or prayer group. Only you and God can see your heart.

I want this book to liberate you, whoever you are, and help you discover your own true self, the _you_ that God created you to be. I want this chapter to help you stop trying to be anyone except yourself. So stop judging yourself because you don't think, look, have, or act like someone else. That person has his or her own story, but so do you. Just like everyone has an individual fingerprint, God has given us each an individual plan.

It's time to look at yours.

My father used to tell me that the decision about who I would marry would be the second most important choice I would ever make, only after my decision to follow Christ. It would affect everything else in my adult life.

"When in doubt, don't," he told me.

I'd long ago memorized Proverbs 18:22 in the original King James version: "Whoso findeth a wife findeth a good thing, and obtaineth favour of the Lord." I'd been waiting my whole life for the right man to "findeth" me. But if this guy I'd promised to marry wasn't on board with who God wanted me to be, was he really God's choice for me?

I prayed for weeks and searched the Scripture for answers. That's when I found what became my favorite verses in the whole Bible, Proverbs 3:5–6: "Trust in the Lord with all your heart, and lean not on your own understanding; in all your ways acknowledge Him, and He shall direct your paths."

I trusted that God had a plan for my future and a direction for my path, but I still wasn't sure what to do about the guy. Three months before the wedding, I went one last time to talk to my fiancé. If he said the right thing, I told my mom, I would stay. But more than I wanted to be married, I wanted to be right with God.

I'll spare you the details of that visit. Let's just say that he didn't say the right thing. I gave him back his ring and called off the wedding. There were lots of tears and heartache and embarrassment, but I knew I was doing the right thing. He was a really nice guy, but he wasn't the right guy. Our relationship had been good, but it wasn't God's design for my life.

Who do you want to be? Who does God want you to be?

Those are hard questions, so let's start with something easier. Do you like eggs?

No, for real.

Getting to know yourself on a deeper level starts with understanding what your "normals" are—you know, those things that you do or think or say because that's what you've always done or thought or said. You never question your normals, because they're what everyone expects you to do. Your normals might be how you and your brother always push each other's buttons, or whether you go to church every week, or how you like to take second helpings of dessert.

One of my girlfriends describes our normals with a story about eggs.

There was a woman who, in her twenties, went with all her girlfriends for brunch every Saturday to eat eggs. "Eggs are the best! Let's always have eggs!" everyone said, and she agreed, even though she wasn't sure whether she really liked eggs that much.

In her thirties, the "eggs for brunch" tradition was firmly established. This was what her friends did every Saturday. And she liked her friends, but by now, she was really tired of eggs. And so she gingerly approached the topic and suggested that they go to the new Mexican restaurant next week, instead. "No, girl! What are you thinking?" her friends all responded. "We do *eggs* on Saturdays!" And so she backed down.

By her forties, though, she'd had it. She'd done the soul work, looked at her normals, and was ready to change. She sat everyone down and said, "I don't like eggs. I don't like the smell or the taste or even the things that we eat with eggs. I don't want to talk about eggs anymore. Next week, it's my choice where we go, and I choose Mexican."

And that's what it took. Her friends heard her, understood her, and agreed. A couple of them even admitted that they were over eggs, too.

So when I ask you about eggs, what I'm really asking is *what are your normals?* What are the things that you say or do because that's what's expected, but are feeling more and more uncomfortable about as time passes?

It's okay to be honest and speak your own truth in love. Instead of trying to live someone else's truth, or match what that person thinks is important, free yourself to be your 100 percent authentic self, the person God created you to be.

This is the root of your spiritual IQ. When you put aside the things that aren't part of you, you open the window to that whisper of the Holy Spirit guiding you to reclaim your past, embrace your present, and prepare for your future.

When you're stuck in your normals, it's easy to let others decide things for you, and that opens the door for the enemy to lead you in the wrong directions. When you don't know what you want, you give up your power to make your own choices. But when you're open to the Holy Spirit and confident in your own place in His universe, your habits no longer own you.

When I was twenty-one, my relationship was my normal. If I would've married the wrong guy, though, I never would have come into the fullness of who God created me to be. If you let the opinions of other people, or the fear of their reactions, define your decisions, you'll miss out, as well.

Let me back up. My calling to sing for God's glory came long before I was engaged.

When I was five, my parents would gather all of us kids in their bedroom, and we would all read Scripture and pray together. Then my mom or dad would ask me to sing for them, and even as a small child I could see the joy that it brought them. I could feel their pride in my efforts. I loved how that felt.

My mom, who played the piano for our church choir, *encouraged me*—okay, she basically made me—start to sing at church, and in time I started to love seeing people praise God with me when I was on stage. At Christmas and Easter, when other kids would get up on stage to give speeches or read Scripture, I would sing.

When I was young, my mom was also singing in a group

with her sisters. They called themselves the Daniels Sisters. I was all of about seven years old when she took me with her to the studio where they were recording a 45, and I thought, "My mommy is a superstar!" I knew right then that this was what I wanted to do.

My parents got on board with my dream right away. My mom even started writing songs specifically for me. By ten years old, I was singing "I'm in Love with the Savior" in churches all over Los Angeles. I like to say it was my first single.

Without really ever asking the question, I knew that God had made me creative, and He called me to His stage. Now it was up to me to obey.

You know how a lot of people tell their kids "you can be whatever you want," or "you can do whatever you want"? Well, one of the pastors at our church tells his children something different. "You cannot be whatever you want to be," he says. "You can be what God has called and chosen you to be."

Of course, his kids *could* try to be whatever they want, but our pastor wants them to know that they won't be as successful without God's favor and blessing and peace, which only comes when we stop trying to bless ourselves and follow our own desires, and instead turn to Him.

God gave you gifts that no one else in the world has in exactly the same way. He put you on this earth for a specific reason, to fill a particular need. But before you can start to live fully within your calling, you need to know what it is.

For some of you, this question is easy. Like me, you've known since you were a kid where your passions would take you. My sister Thomasina, who we all call Goo Goo, has always been excited about fashion and clothes, and she's worked hard to follow that dream and build it into a career. You might be gifted in the area of health and wellness, and your heart beats faster when you have the chance to help someone who's sick or injured. You might be good at creating a place where people feel warm and welcome, and you feel happiest when you make others feel comfortable. You might be a teacher, always bringing truth and knowledge to the conversation. You might be a visionary, able to see what should come next. You might be a helper, gifted to provide tireless support and keep things running smoothly.

Whatever your area is, your heart lights up when you follow it.

You might be reading this, though, and not have any idea what your calling is. You don't know what your gift is. You might never have even asked the question before. Life's crowded enough just trying to get by—paying the bills and getting the kids to school and taking care of the million and one things on your list every day. It's easier to settle into the mundane, familiar tracks of your life. Do what everyone else does. Don't rock the boat. Who has time for a calling?

You do. Or at least, you should. Romans 11:29 says, "For the gifts and the calling of God are irrevocable." And in Ephesians

4:1, Paul says, "I therefore, the prisoner for the Lord, beseech you to walk worthy of the calling with which you were called."

There's no such thing as a small calling, or a gift that doesn't matter. Most of us won't start a school in South Africa like Oprah, or run for Congress, or share our testimony in front of millions. Some of the most spiritually powerful and influential women I know have never traveled beyond their own city. But if you let God work His desires through you, I guarantee you will make a difference in the circle He's given you.

Living in your calling brings a spark into your life. It gives you meaning and points you toward the people and activities that make you feel fulfilled, happy, and full of purpose.

If you've never stopped to identify your calling, here's a place to start.

Sit in the quiet with a pen and paper, and ask yourself, *What makes my heart sing? Have I talked to God about whether that's connected to His plans for me?*

Write down your answers, and sort out your thoughts the old-fashioned way, on paper. You'll see yourself in a new light when you have to put your ideas into words, but don't spend time overthinking this. Write the first things that come to your mind.

What are your gifts?

What are the things that you're better than most at doing, that excite you, that bring joy to you and to others?

Where is God blessing you?

Where is He leading you?

It might be hard at first to think about those places where you're gifted. I once heard a pastor talk about this, and he explained that it's easy for us to get stuck on trying to fix the things about ourselves that are bad. We pay attention to what needs to be improved. _Where am I vulnerable to temptation? How can I be better?_ And there's a place for that. You need to be vigilant about the places where you're getting off track. But it's also good to set aside time to recognize and celebrate the things that God has gifted in you. Acknowledge what you want to work on, but also tell yourself what's good. Be real with yourself about the blessings and strengths that you have to work with. It's okay to have a personal party every now and then.

In fact, those celebrations might just lead you to a breakthrough.

Once you're done writing, go back and read what you've said, and bring it to God in prayer. Ask Him to show you what's important, and what He wants you to see. Where are the points where the things that excite you overlap with the needs of the world around you?

Remember, your calling is not always the same as your job. For a long time, before Mary Mary started, I made money working in a salon doing hair in order to pay the bills. That was my job, but not my calling.

Paying the bills is important, and I'm never going to tell you to ignore your job or do it poorly if your calling is somewhere else. You should honor yourself and your community by being responsible with your commitments. But if you're spending all of your time and energy on a job that leaves you dry and dusty, dissatisfied with God and your situation, you're trapped without purpose. God created you for more than drudgery. He created you for destiny.

When you look at your list, you may also have a moment where you compare what you find to what you see in someone else. Don't do that. Comparison kills! We all have our own gifts. If you waste time trying to live up to someone else's gift, you're always going to come up short. That's not because there's anything lacking in you, but because what you're looking at is not what God has set aside for you. When you envy what someone else can do, you stop trying to be you. You stop resting in who God called you to be.

Nothing insults God more than you acting like who you are and what you are isn't good enough, because it was He who gave you everything you need to be everything that He wants you to be.

As I like to tell my radio listeners, God doesn't do anything for you without you. He's not going to take you to your places of blessing without your participation. It's up to you to first find out what you were meant to do, and then to find the way to live it out.

Understanding that I was called to a career in music didn't mean I automatically knew how to get there.

When I was in high school, I thought I was everything because I was a part of my awesome church's choir. The Evangelistic Church of God in Christ Mass Choir won first place at the 1990 McDonald's Gospelfest and even recorded an album. If I knew you back then, I was quick to tell you that honey, we were a *thing* in Los Angeles.

But as graduation got closer, my questions got bigger. My dreams got bigger. How did a person go from being a girl in a choir to a professional singer?

One of my older cousins, Frankie, held a special role in our extended family at the time. Whenever someone was getting ready to graduate, Frankie would take them for a drive, one on one, and ask what that person wanted to become. He'd listen to us, help us think about our futures, and encourage us toward college.

When it was my turn, Frankie took me for my drive and asked what I was good at. I told him I was good at singing, and I wanted a career on stage.

"Okay," he said, "so go to school for singing."

Until he said that, I didn't even know that music was something you could study in school. But with his encouragement, I enrolled in college for vocal studies, and using what I learned there, I started to sing.

By the time that my ill-fated engagement ended, I was singing all over the city. Community festivals, local business openings, radio station events—I would go anywhere. I didn't make any money from it at first, but I knew in my heart that my work was building me toward something greater. I went from church to church, place to place, singing for anyone who would listen. And every time, I would ask God, *Is this the time? Is today the day that I will meet the right person?* I was sure it would be like what I saw in the movies, when someone in the audience would see me and say, "That face! That voice!"

There was a night when a famous record producer was at an event where I was singing, and I thought, *This is it. He's going to hear me and sign me tonight, right now, to his label.* Nope. That didn't happen. And so I kept singing.

And then one night, Warryn Campbell walked into my life.

Why did I want to be a singer? Was it to see the pride and joy on the faces of my parents? To stand out from the crowd of kids and family and church members who surrounded me? Or was it to share the joy and wonder of what Jesus had brought into my life?

Those were questions I had to ask myself over and over as I moved toward my calling. I had to keep checking in with my soul to make sure that I was doing the right things for the right reasons. And as God brought me into new places and I faced new challenges, that same question of "why" came up again and again. In my marriage, in my family, in my career, and now as a mom, I've asked a lot of whys. And every time, God has used that exercise to give me a new perspective.

If you want to really know who you are, you can't skip over the why. I believe that why is the most important question that

God's given you, because *why* is the tool that helps you dig below the surface of a situation and see where your reactions to it come from.

Why do you feel the way you do? Did that person's words hurt your feelings because you were already feeling low self-esteem? Why are you in this relationship, or that situation? Why do you want to avoid being around people right now, or why is it so hard for you to be alone? If you're unhappy or dissatisfied, why do you feel that way?

And don't just ask *why* about your own thoughts and actions. When you're stuck in a conflict with another person, *why* is the question to help you through it. If someone hurt you, why did they act the way they did? Why did they lose their temper so fast? Is there something happening in their life, apart from you, that set them off? Were you in the wrong place at the wrong time?

Asking *why* will help you understand yourself better, but it isn't always going to bring up answers you like. At some point, you'll have to face your well of brokenness, that place where past hurts and doubts have carved out dark holes in your memories. You may need to revisit and reconsider some old ideas. But just the act of looking at painful things with an open and curious mind, not with shame or guilt, will bring new light and fresh air to them. You'll start to see your story in a new way.

A lot of women I talk to get stuck on this question of why. They use it as a reason to start throwing blame or make excuses. "Why am I feeling bad about my relationship? Well, because my boyfriend does this or my mom says that." No. This isn't about them. It's about you. Why do *you* respond the way you do? If someone acts so bad, why do you put up with it? Why have you given that person power over how you respond? Could self-control be the lesson you're supposed to learn?

If there are things that you're afraid of or avoid, ask why. Maybe you went to a teacher years ago for help and were dismissed or rejected. Is that why it's hard to ask for help now? A lot of our fears come from past experiences where we were shut down. One of my sisters saw an important music executive in the airport once and went up to say hello. The response he gave her was so cold that she refused to approach anyone with an ounce of fame for years. But understanding the rejection she felt helped her to get past it.

Asking God to reveal to you the truth of your situation takes courage, it takes commitment, and it takes a lot of work. But you have to do the work to get to the better part of you.

Back to when I met Warryn. I'd been putting myself out there, over and over, for years. There were so many times when I thought about giving up. It would have been so much easier to get one of those "normal" jobs. But I didn't quit. I had the support of my family and my church, and I learned more with every event, even from the rejections—and there were loads of rejections.

In 1994, I was cast in a role in a touring musical. I talked Tina into auditioning, too, and so that was the first time the Atkins sisters traveled and performed backgrounds together. Most of our lives, I was a solo lead singer. It's hard to imagine this now, watching us as Mary Mary, but when we were younger I was the outgoing one, and Tina was the shy one. I was the lead singer in church, but she had to be pushed to take the front of the stage. Oh, how times have changed.

We were on the road for five months and had just gotten back to California when an up-and-coming music producer happened to attend the show.

Warryn says that as soon as he saw me on that stage, he was hooked. I don't know about that, but I do know that he got his cousin and his dad to come to the show with him the next night. After the show, he approached me, we started talking, he asked for my number, and things started happening.

He says that I blew him off that first night, but that's not how I remember it. I thought he was cute but really young—Warryn's three years younger than me, and I was used to dating older guys. But the more we talked, the more I liked how much we had in common. Our energy matched, we both grew up in church, and okay, I'll admit I quickly got a little obsessed with his smile.

Unlike my previous fiancé, Warryn never questioned my calling. In fact, he encouraged it. He was already making a name for himself in the music industry, working with names I recognized in R&B and hip-hop, and so we talked about music as a profession all the time. I didn't tell him at first how I felt called to sing on my own, though, because I never wanted him to think that I was spending time with him so that he'd help my career. I really, really liked this guy for himself.

Finally, one day, I was lightly mentioning some work that I'd done, and he turned to me and asked, "You really, really want this music career, don't you?" I said yes, and that's when he started getting involved.

It was Warryn's idea for us to form Mary Mary. Tina and I were always together, and so he'd heard us sing together casually, and then she shared with him some of the songs we'd "made up." We didn't even know to call ourselves songwriters yet! He liked what he heard, and with his help, Tina and I got a publishing deal with EMI and started writing professionally. We wrote and performed on soundtracks for movies like *Stuart Little*, *Dr. Doolittle*, and *The Prince of Egypt*, and we toured individually and together as backup singers for R&B singers like Brandy, Brian McKnight, Kenny Lattimore, and Eric Benét.

Then in 1997, we wrote a song called "Shackles," and that changed all of our lives.

God's promises were kept, and our persistence was rewarded, just as I always knew it would be.

In the Bible, Job was a man who had once been successful. He had money, he had influence, and he had a big family. But God let the enemy take everything from him.

If there was ever a man with a reason to doubt himself, it was Job. But in chapter 42, in the middle of his suffering, he told

God, "I know that You can do everything, and that no purpose of Yours can be withheld from You." Now that's confidence, to understand that God's plan is bigger than any circumstance.

Confidence is something I talk about a lot on my radio show and in my public speaking, because I would never have made it to these places in life without being certain of who I am and what God wanted from me. Confidence in God's plan, remember, is different than ego. I didn't do any of this on my own. I *can't* do any of this on my own. No matter what, my confidence rests in this: I am always a child of God, and my future rests not in what I can do, but in what He can do through me. Confidence in Him means being assured that He's in control, and that if I'm in line with Him, I'm on the right path.

What about you? Are you confident in who you are as a child of God? Do you believe that the Holy Spirit guides you, and do you trust that if you're obedient He will lead you in the right directions and protect you when the enemy attacks?

Confidence like that grows out of the soul work of knowing yourself. It's the ability to feel beautiful, smart, and successful without needing someone else to say it. It's the wisdom to recognize the danger of offers that look good on the surface but aren't in line with the plan God has for you.

It's hard for the enemy to sway the mind of a confident woman. Her power doesn't come from her own willpower, but from Christ's perfect power. She responds to temptation with, "No, thanks. That's not who I am."

I shared in the last chapter that an ego-driven self-confidence is fickle, dependent on emotions and circumstances. When things are going badly, your ego's confidence collapses. When things are going well, it can make you arrogant. A God-centered confidence, on the other hand, never changes. The shifting sands of the world around it don't affect the landscape.

When we look at how Jesus lived on earth, we see an example of this godly confidence. Jesus always knew who He was and what His purpose was. "I must work the works of Him that sent Me," He said. But He never let that confidence become arrogance. He never swaggered into a room and demanded a donkey or fresh water. Instead, He lived in total humility. He was a perfect example of fully human and fully divine.

Jesus didn't flaunt His calling, and so I don't flaunt mine, either. I'm the fullness of Erica whether I'm at the grocery store or all glammed up for the red carpet, whether I have makeup on or I'm home washing dishes. Because I am sure of *who* I am, my environment doesn't dictate *how* I am. I can take the compliments and the awards and still remember, *Erica, you're a servant of the most high God. Don't get too pumped up. Don't believe the hype. They're seeing what's on stage and what's on TV, but they don't see you when the wig's off and you're at home. They see your house looking nice on the show, but they don't know about all the stuff that's piled in the laundry room.*

Every day, I remind myself that my career is based on God's timing and divine intervention. He chose me for this. I wouldn't be here if God didn't have a purpose and a plan for my music ministry to bless people. Like Job, I could watch everything material disappear overnight. But that hasn't happened. God hasn't said that it's finished, and so my confidence rests in the knowledge that He's not finished, so I'm not finished.

The world wants you to think that confidence is "fake it 'til you make it," but that kind of false behavior is shallow and doesn't last. When your confidence is only skin deep, your conscience knows that you're relying on your ego, and that you're a fraud. You invite fear into your life, because there's always that feeling that you might get caught.

Fear is the opposite of confidence. In 2 Timothy 1:7, the apostle says, "For God has not given us a spirit of fear, but of power and of love and of a sound mind." Fear is the enemy's tool to distract and dissuade you, and it has no place in your life. When you know yourself and are in tune with the Holy Spirit's guidance, there's no room for fear.

So if there's a place in your life where fear fills you, go back to that earlier section about asking *why* and dig in. Why do you feel fear? What is the story from your past or the message in your mind that pushes you to that feeling? And how can you gather your spiritual confidence to push that feeling right off your lap? Listen, it's not sinful to feel fear or to struggle with doubt or unbelief. The Scripture tells us that we can be honest and pray the prayer of a desperate father in Mark 9: "Lord, I believe; help my unbelief!"

When I tell my kids, "Don't get scared, get ready," what I'm really telling them is to find their confidence and hold onto it. And it's a good reminder for you, too. Prepare your spirit, prepare your mind, and believe that you will overcome and that you already have the victory.

Once things started happening for Mary Mary, they happened fast. Our writing and music caught the attention of two record labels, and Tina, Warryn, and I flew to New York to meet with them. We traveled on our own dime and shared a single hotel room because we barely had a nickel between us, but it was important to us not to be obligated to anyone. After lots of prayer and meetings, Mary Mary signed with Columbia.

"Shackles" shot up the Billboard charts and hit the top five in a bunch of countries, and suddenly everyone was talking about this new gospel duo. Our debut album, *Thankful*, won a Grammy for Best Gospel Album in 2001. Tina and I went from being two sisters who could barely afford the rent to turning on the radio and hearing our own voices playing back to us. We toured the world—London, Brazil, Japan, Madrid, Germany . . . the countries all started to blend together.

I was twenty-eight, Tina was twenty-six, and the whole world just opened up to us.

"Shackles" ended up being a crossover hit, getting attention and airplay from a lot of listeners who don't usually go for gospel music. One of them, a music industry executive who will remain anonymous, approached Tina and me not long after that first

Grammy. He told us that we were sexy and had great voices, and if we wanted to shift from singing gospel to R&B, we could get a million-dollar deal.

A million dollars is a lot to anyone, but for two middle sisters used to dollar-store shopping, it was crazy.

"More fans will love you," the executive said. "Just take the Jesus stuff out. Sing about good things and nice things. Say 'him' if you're getting religious."

Just take Jesus out? That stopped the conversation. "Shackles" was a gospel song, after all, and it went platinum. We loved singing gospel and had no desire to be anything but gospel singers. And so we told the industry executive that taking Jesus out wasn't an option.

I still shake my head when I think about how God gave us the opportunity to turn down the chance at a million-dollar contract. The enemy must have seen how much more was coming.

Over and over, you will be tested. The enemy will come at you with whatever he can, digging at your weak spot or the place of your biggest need.

Are you ready? Do you know yourself well enough to know what's right and wrong for you? Have you spoken for yourself enough to speak up for what really matters? Do you have a voice? Are you using it?

It seems weird to say this now, when everyone knows I talk for hours every morning on the radio, but for a long time, I struggled to find my own voice. In my family, everyone else always had something to say. In church, everyone had an opinion. My world was full of color and life . . . and noise. It took effort to be heard in a space like that, so I told myself that I was happy to let others have the spotlight.

Even in Mary Mary, no one seemed to know my real name. I was always just "one of the Marys" or "one of the girls," and I was fine with that. There were only two of us, so I had the chance to shine and to do the music I wanted, but the group name meant that I didn't really need to publicly establish who I was as a person.

Tina had grown from her shy self into quite a talker, and so I let her handle things. I never felt the need to push in conversations. If anyone asked me for an opinion, I'd say, "Oh, whatever you think is fine." If anyone pushed me on it, I would say that I wasn't assertive.

I hated to argue or come off as confrontational, and I'm not alone. There are a lot of you reading this book today who would describe yourself as "shy" if someone called on you to share more than you wanted to.

Shy is fear's first cousin. Shy happens when people are afraid to put themselves out there or worry about the results. Shy says "expressing myself is dangerous."

God calls us to be bold and stand out front. He calls us to proclaim Him and to live openly as His followers. 1 Peter 3:15 says, "Always be ready to give a defense to everyone who asks you a reason for the hope that is in you."

God doesn't do anything for you without you. He wants you to have a voice and a place in your own story.

Mary Mary recorded, toured, and ministered together full time. Tina and I recorded eight albums, won four Grammys, and starred in six seasons of our reality show. During that time, we both got married and had our kids—three for me and five for her. Those were busy, happy, hard years.

People loved Mary Mary. We were well known and accepted, and I was happy to sit back and sing until God decided it was time to give me a chance to find my own voice.

In 2013, Tina and I decided that it was time to pursue our own projects for a while. Mary Mary wasn't breaking up, we told the world (and ourselves), but we would explore other opportunities.

God does stuff like that if He sees you getting too comfortable, too complacent. He'll shake things up. He'll offer you the opportunity to grow, and then wait to see if you're willing to take it.

Becoming a solo artist was an enormous opportunity, but it also brought a lot of questions. If my own name was on the cover of an album, what did I want to say? Who did I want to be when I was interviewed on my own?

Everywhere I went, I realized, people were listening to me, and I enjoyed it.

I'd been following the soul work journey I've described. I'd tackled my ego and shifted my normals to match His desires, and I'd asked a lot of why questions. I was starting to find my voice, and to believe that I had something of value to say. God had already stretched me, and now He had a platform for me that exceeded anything I'd dreamed for myself.

Stepping out on my own changed my entire life. I discovered layers of confidence. I realized my words were necessary. I started to ask God not just what He wanted me to do, but what He wanted me to say. All of a sudden, I was talking all the time, to everyone.

For years, I'd toyed with the desire to do radio. I loved talking to people and interviewing my friends in the entertainment industry about their music or movies or books.

In 2015, I went to a meeting with a number of other gospel music artists and influencers to talk about the state of gospel radio and how we could reach our audience in new and better ways. I was long past the shy, quiet, "no, whatever you want is fine" days, and so I spoke my heart in that room.

The next day, I got a call from Cathy Hughes, the owner of Urban One, the biggest broadcaster of African-American content in the country. She'd heard what I said the day before, and she wanted to know if I was interested in doing a daily syndicated morning show. Those conversations quickly led to a new program, a new studio in Dallas, and a whole lot of time spent on airplanes.

Today, I mostly record from home, starting at three in the morning, California time. Yes, I'm tired, but it's worth it. God gave me a platform bigger than I'd ever dreamed to share the things that are near and dear to my heart, and the opportunity to connect with and interview people I have admired for years. Things most people can only discuss in small rooms, I can share with the world. Most of all, He's given me the blessing of talking to everyday people who call me from all over the country to ask for prayer and advice about tough issues in their lives.

Something happens when you do the soul work of discovering yourself. You start to find that you have something to say after all. When you know what you believe, what makes you special, and how you're called, something inside you comes alive. You feel the urge to open your mouth and claim your space in the world.

That's what happens when you ask God to give you a voice.

Now it's your turn. Your words have power. Your words have value. There's someone in your life who needs to hear you. There's someone who needs exactly what you have to say.

If that idea is still uncomfortable to you, don't sit in your corner and second-guess yourself. Don't tell yourself nobody will listen. Go back to that mirror and keep looking. Keep reminding yourself what God sees. Keep asking yourself why. You'll get there.

Our God is too powerful to leave you afraid of your own thoughts and feelings, if you're willing to be honest and trust Him. He loves you too much to leave you in silence. He made you to be someone important, someone worth hearing.

Chapter 6

Let Go

Whe Krista was little, Warryn and I recognized that she was very verbal, as well as smart and beautiful, and so we got her an agent and started going to auditions. That's just what you do when you're a parent in Los Angeles. Krista wasn't cast for anything, though. Directors don't always pick the brown-skinned children, or the kids who are a little heavier. Hollywood is tough, and my daughter heard her share of no.

One day when she was about seven, I drove her to yet another audition. Before we got out of the car, I asked if she wanted to pray. Krista bowed her head and jumped right in. "Lord, I thank you for my talent," she said. "I thank you for my mommy taking me here, and I hope I get the part. But Lord, if I don't, it's their loss and not mine."

I sat there, my eyes filled with tears. *Lord, please let her carry that attitude with her throughout her life. Let her understand that if someone doesn't want to be her friend, it's that person's loss. If somebody doesn't want to be kind, it's not a reflection of who she is and how amazing she is. Because God, this is one amazing kid.*

While she was in her audition, I called all of my sisters to tell them that my Krista, at seven, was a smart girl. She'd already figured out what a lot of adults I know still struggle with: that who we are—our value and potential and beauty—does not depend on the people around us. If someone hurts us, or disappoints us, or gets angry with us, it does not change our reflections in God's mirror.

I like to tell my kids that if someone calls me a purple buffalo, that doesn't mean that I am a purple buffalo. We don't have to turn our lives upside down to prove that I'm not a purple buffalo. We don't have to start a fight to change the mind of the person who says I'm a purple buffalo. As long as what others think doesn't disturb the way we live our lives, we can let them have their silly thoughts. Let them draw pictures of me as a purple buffalo. Let them even laugh at it. We don't give them our energy if they don't deserve it.

That truth can be hard to put into practice, though. By the time you grow up, you've probably had your heart broken, your loyalty tested, and your respect challenged a time or ten. Someone along the way did something a lot more serious than calling you a purple buffalo.

Those disappointments can weigh your spirit down for years if you let them, but they don't have to. Over and over in Scripture, you'll find that God does not want you to linger in places of pain. Ephesians 3:17–19 tells us that God's desire is for us to be "rooted and grounded in love . . . able to comprehend with all the saints what is the width and length and depth and height—to know the love of Christ which passes knowledge; that you may be filled with all the fullness of God."

It's time for some tough talk about the soul work of letting go, because you can't be everything God wants you to be until you stop holding onto the pieces of your story that don't point to Him.

When you took stock of yourself in the last chapter, especially if you stopped to really ask yourself the *why* questions, you may have noticed that certain events from your past kept coming up. Maybe there was some tough stuff that happened to you that changed the way you saw the world, and maybe still affects the way you act with others.

For me, it was my parents' marriage. I told you before that my parents married and divorced each other three times while I was growing up. My dad always told us that my mom was the love of his life, but that didn't stop him from leaving when things got hard. And his inconsistent presence left me with a lot of questions and insecurity that I carried all the way through my teen years and into my own marriage.

When I look back, I understand why my parents had such a messy relationship. They loved each other deeply, but they could never figure out how to communicate effectively, and their disagreements were all harder with a bunch of kids to take care of and not enough money to make ends meet.

My dad had been in the military, which had made him very

structured. He wanted hospital corners on the sheets of every bed, and he taught all of us kids the "right way" to wipe the table after a meal—always right to left, starting at one end and moving to the other, never swiping back over a place the rag had been. He always dressed sharp, with his pants creased and his shirt tucked in. If he needed to be somewhere at a certain time, he planned it all out to the minute.

My mom, on the other hand, was more of a free spirit. She wanted to go with the flow. Even today, she tries to squeeze a lot of things into every day for her and everyone else, so she tends to be a little late. My mom poured herself into our family, but sometimes that challenged her marriage. Now, my mom never bashed my dad in front of us, and she welcomed him back without a negative word every time he returned. We were all happy when Daddy came home. But she definitely had her own ideas about how things should be done.

The time I remember most is when my dad announced one Sunday during our church service that he was starting a new church. It was the first time any of his kids had heard about it, and we all just sat there with smiles pasted on our faces to hide our confusion. Well, once the church was started we went and sang a few times, but my mom didn't really help out much, because she said she wanted to keep her kids in the church where we were already active and comfortable. We never heard them argue about it, but I know they did, and before long my dad was packing again.

No matter how many times my dad told me he loved me, I

grew up believing that love wasn't enough to keep him, or by default any man, near me. And it wasn't just me who believed that. Some of the women in my community did everything they could to "prepare" me for what they thought relationships were like. "Honey, make sure you have your own job and your own money, because you never know when he's going to go," said one. "And live close to your mama in case something happens," another added. When I was engaged, one woman told me flat out, "You don't live in a fairy tale anymore. Get ready for the real world."

Looking back, I can see the hurt in those women's words. I get how their disappointments and experiences wove into blankets of self-preservation that they wore like shields and offered to younger women like me as an ill-considered kindness. But their pain prepared us for nothing but another generation of broken families.

My experience left me stuck, unable to trust my own relationships. But slowly, God guided me through this soul work and I learned to release those suspicious ideas. You see, God taught me that lasting love is possible if it's God's design for love. That's not easy—it means being forgiving and patient, and opening yourself and observing what's really happening with another person instead of trying to protect your heart all the time. It means praying to love a person and see that person through God's eyes.

I always wanted my dad to pour himself out over his family, but I've come to understand that he loved me and gave me all he had, even if it wasn't all that I wanted. Step by step, as I grew, the Holy Spirit led me to a place where I could understand my family's brokenness.

"I wanted my family," my dad told me in his later years, when he was near the end of his life and filled with regret for his early impulsive choices. "I want you to know that. I always came back, because my family is what I really wanted. I didn't know how to fix it or fix your mom, but I really tried."

I cried when he said that. Thirty years before, that would have been hard for me to accept, but today, I'm convinced that it's true. My father loved us the best that he could, and that's all I can ask from anyone.

Is there a similar story of disappointment or brokenness that's weighing you down? Maybe you didn't get to go to the prom because your family couldn't afford the ticket or a dress. Maybe your dad or mom left your family and never came back. Maybe someone didn't show up for you when you needed that person. Maybe those kids in school did terrible things to you. Maybe a boyfriend or a date did something to crush your spirit. Maybe you were sexually abused.

How do you handle that memory today? Does it still haunt you? Do you still hold a grudge?

When pain lingers for years or even decades, a lot of people start to treat it like a pet. They feed it and groom it and keep it on their laps. They're always aware of its presence. Their pain, in other words, defines them. *I'm a victim*, they say. *I can't do this thing that God says to do, or be there for that person who needs me, because I've been hurt.*

It's time to put a stop to that kind of thinking. It's dangerous to put your pain above God.

I'm not dismissing your past, or saying that your feelings aren't real. I may not have met you, but I know you've been through some stuff, because we all have. But I want to be clear that your pain doesn't have to be with you forever. You can learn to keep the memory and not the pain.

Pain expands to fill the spaces you give it, and it blocks you from fully living in God's blessing. The hard things in your past can distract you from the amazing things God has in your future. Pain draws all of your attention inward until the only person you can see is yourself.

There were moments in your life that left you with scars, but scars eventually heal. When I was eight years old, I burned my arm on an exposed heater, and it left a mark. I used to sit in school and stare at that scar for hours, thinking that it looked like the White House and the Capitol building combined. Today, I can barely see where it was.

Scars will fade if you don't pick at them. Pain will heal if you don't claim it. And that story that fills you with hurt or anger today will slide away into your history if you don't keep rehearsing it and reliving the circumstances.

The offenses in your past don't have to lead to bitterness. They don't have to distract you or make you cynical about the future. The people who hurt you were human beings with their own messy histories, temptations, and battles to fight. Yet God loves them just as much as He loves you, and He forgives them just the same as He forgives you. So if their stuff spilled over and affected your life, or if they gave you the best they could but it wasn't everything you needed, it's time to let God's forgiveness and love consume you. Bring your story to God and ask Him to help you release it. He will redeem every part of your past and change anything that's in your heart if you ask Him.

Just so we're clear: letting go is not the same as sweeping your feelings under the rug. Pain that is unaddressed is just as damaging as pain that is too often expressed. Repressed feelings end up coming out eventually, often when we least expect them. They explode either internally or externally.

I remember watching a press conference at the end of a big sports event, and the star player was at the podium, thanking everyone. He thanked his coach, and his teammates, and his wife. "None of this would be possible without her," he said passionately, with tears in his eyes. Then the camera panned to her, and I could see that she was just a ball of tension. Her arms were crossed. In the middle of an emotional celebration, she wasn't even cracking a smile. All I could think was that this was a woman whose heart was not in that room. She was somewhere else, caught up in the pain of something else.

If you've been hurt, the enemy can use the hole left by your pain to fill you with a spirit of rejection. He'll curl around you and whisper messages of self-pity and worthlessness into your ears and infiltrate your soul. He will tell you that you're unwanted and mistreated.

In Chapter 2, we talked about how we can invite negative spirits into our lives and onto our laps, though they do nothing but harm us. Rejection is another one of those. Rejection attacks your understanding of how you fit in the world.

When you spend your quiet time feeling sorry for yourself, and you truly believe that no one in the whole world likes you, you're welcoming the spirit of rejection onto your lap and letting it, not God, direct your future. If you always feel like you're on the outside of a conversation, if you're easily offended and slow to forgive, or if you give up easily, those are signs that you're battling the spirit of rejection. If you go into new situations expecting to be unheard or think no one understands you, or you believe that your problems are bigger than anyone else's in the world, then the enemy's lies are blocking your path toward God's plan.

God does not reject you, nor does He want you to feel rejected. Psalm 94:14 says, "For the Lord will not cast off His people, nor will He forsake His inheritance." His love is freely given, and His desire is to bless you with His fullness. His message to you is always the same: you are loved. You are full of purpose, and are an important part of His creation and plan. But He will only show you the way if you do your part, which is to come out of agreement with the things that are not from Him.

You have the power to send the rejection that you're feeling back to the negative dark hole it came from.

How? That's where the soul work comes in. Start by asking the Holy Spirit to alert you to the poisonous words that you have been speaking over your life, and repent from the word curses you've already spoken. Search His word for His promises, and commit daily to seeing other people—even the difficult ones—through His eyes, rather than your own expectation or comparison. Forgive those who offended you, and release your judgment over others, because that's bouncing back and causing you to be judged.

When someone insults you or tries to bring you down, whether it's in person or online, don't hold onto it. Let it go. That person's words are not a reflection of who you really are or who God made you to be. Even if another person is burdened under his or her own negativity, you still have a choice.

In other words, just because someone calls you a purple buffalo doesn't mean that you are a purple buffalo. You don't have to believe them.

I don't get sad, Erica. I get angry. Yeah, I hear you. You're not alone. We live in a world that rewards conflict and complaining. People get mad on social media. They get mad in their cars when they're stuck in traffic. They get mad when they watch cable news. They get mad when they listen to certain kinds of music that encourage anger. They even get mad at church.

I can be just as guilty of letting my temper go as anyone else. In our years of working together, Tina and I have been mad at each other plenty of times. What can I say? We're two strong women trying to balance careers and family dynamics, and we don't always see eye to eye. We have our ups and downs. She's my sister and I love her, but we've fought with each other right up to the second we walked out onto a stage or into a big media interview. And yeah, I've shouted a time or two.

And Tina's not the only person who has experienced my anger.

There are days when I get mad at the comments and opinions on social media, and I have to sit on my hands to keep from responding. I'm a tough chick from Inglewood, California, after all, and sometimes I want to tell people all the way off. People challenge me, or they come at me with wrong information, and I want to stand up for myself. I want to defend myself with a little sass and sarcasm, or at least politely insult them. I want to casually list my awards and accomplishments to the haters and the doubters. There have definitely been days when Warryn has had to say in love, "You need to erase that comment, First Lady Erica Campbell of Mary Mary, woman of God. You were called to minister, not to clap back."

And yeah, he's usually right. We've seen time after time how easy it is for the enemy to use and manipulate believers' words when they try to "defend themselves" on a public forum. Being under scrutiny comes with the territory—not just of being in the music industry, but of being a follower of Jesus. 2 Timothy 2:23–25 reminds me that I need to "avoid foolish and ignorant disputes, knowing that they generate strife. A servant of the

Lord must not quarrel but be gentle to all, able to teach, patient, in humility correcting those who are in opposition."

But still, I've raised my voice with my kids. I've been mad at friends. I've held bitterness in my heart from stories I heard secondhand, quotes without context. I've held relationships hostage for years while I made my pain my pet. I've told people I love, "Forget it, let's just not talk ever again," even though that's not what my heart meant. I was just letting my pain speak for me.

Anger itself isn't wrong. It's a true emotion, and God understands that we'll experience it. Remember, Jesus was filled with some righteous fury in the temple when He turned over the money changers' tables and started yelling about the den of thieves.

In Ephesians 4:26, Paul paraphrases the Psalms when he says "Be angry, and do not sin: do not let the sun go down on your wrath." And James writes, "So then, my beloved brethren, let every man be swift to hear, slow to speak, slow to wrath." The writers don't tell us to *deny* our anger, but to *control* it. "For the wrath of man does not produce the righteousness of God," James continues. There are things that will make you mad, but don't stay mad. It's all about self-control.

Anger, like pain, is something to experience, name, and then let go. Why? Because it's hard to focus your energy on an argument and worship God at the same time. Anger is a poison that sucks up all of your energy and pulls your attention away from your true purpose and calling. The enemy uses your distraction as an opportunity to flood you with other damaging spirits like revenge, bitterness, and jealousy, which all leave holes burning in your heart if you allow them to linger.

So don't carry the spirit of offense. Don't let something keep you burdened. Those people who made your blood boil? Throwing insults and calling names won't change them. Proverbs 15:1 says, "A soft answer turns away wrath, but a harsh word stirs up anger." Only God can change people, and He's not going to do that through your flaming messages on social media, or your ugly words when you run into them at Target.

If there's a situation in your life right now that leaves you steaming, it's time to talk to the Holy Spirit. Step away from your feelings of outrage and ask with an open mind if the situation is worth your energy and attention. Is there really an issue here, or are you reacting to someone else's feelings? Is there something good or beneficial that can come from the conflict, or is it time to release the situation and turn your attention back to things that really matter? Everything doesn't have to be a fight. Every fight doesn't have to be fought. Sometimes, it's not worth stirring up your soul.

If your conflict involves a situation that does matter, then seek the Holy Spirit's guidance in whether you have a responsibility toward reconciliation. Is it possible to step back in order to try again with a more peaceful attitude? Could a calm, rational conversation help both of you release the feelings and refocus on what matters? Maybe you need to offer that "soft answer" in the form of an apology for the places where you know you were wrong. Write a note or send an email. Send flowers. Do what you have to do to get that dangerous anger out of your heart.

There's always the possibility that it's all a misunderstanding. I've seen so many relationships—work relationships, personal relationships, spiritual relationships, and whole churches—come to an end because someone thinks that someone else said something. Feelings get hurt over actions that never happened, or didn't happen the way we think.

For years, I held a grudge against that usher in church who I thought was talking about me. I let her words hit my heart and shape my life. Every time I saw her, the memory would eat at me, even as I pasted on a respectful smile and said hello because she was my elder. Only now, years later, am I wondering if it was all a misunderstanding.

If something seems bad, take the time to communicate without being quarrelsome. Pray before you go, and take the Holy Spirit with you so that you say the right thing, but ask the hard questions. "Hey, did you really say . . . ?" That's not the same as going up and getting in the person's face and throwing down an "I heard you said . . ." Remember, there's a good chance that you'll find out that what you heard isn't what happened. Or at least, it's not everything that happened. Life is usually more complicated than the story you hear at first.

Even if the other person won't engage, do the soul work to live your own best life and turn your focus back to forgiveness. God does not hold you responsible for the decisions or actions of others. Don't let the situation weigh you down. Especially if there is value in the relationship, don't hold onto a grudge until you're eighty years old and it's too late.

No matter how mad Tina and I get at each other, we're always family, and we're always Mary Mary. We work together. We serve the Lord together. We celebrate our lives together. We are sisters and we love each other, and time after time, we put aside our disagreements and focus on what we're called to do, because we both know that we can't be soldiers in the army of the Lord if we're spending all of our time being angry and emotional.

Okay, it's time to get real. I tell you my stories not because I want you to think I'm some great example of a perfect life, but because I want you to understand that I'm not spewing facts from a place that I haven't been. I'm not giving you information that I didn't have to live first. And so if we're going to talk about how I learned about letting go, I have to tell you about the hardest time of all, the day when my husband came home and said, "I need to talk to you."

That didn't seem good. I was on tour at the time, and just passing through our house for what's called a "refresh"—unpack, repack, and go again. I knew that things in my marriage had been distant, but I wasn't ready for what came next.

"I have two questions," I said. "Are you leaving? Are you cheating?"

He couldn't meet my eyes. "Well, I'm not leaving."

That's how I found out about my husband's infidelity.

When Warryn asked my dad for permission to marry me, my dad said, "Good, Erica needs someone to take care of her." I was in my mid-twenties by then, and when Warryn told me about the conversation, I was like, "What? I don't need anyone to take care of me."

Whether I realized it or not, I entered my marriage with all of those messages about not trusting a man still ringing in my ears. I loved my new husband, but I thought I needed to take care of myself. My music career was taking off and I was on the road a lot, and Warryn was working in the studio for days at a time. After we had Krista, all of my extra attention was on taking care of my daughter, and my new husband became third on my list.

Still, I never saw it coming.

Everyone always says that they never expect infidelity to invade their marriage, and I was no different. I thought we were above all of that. We were Christians, active in our church, working for the Lord. But the enemy knows our weak spots, and my absence—both emotional and physical—created a hole that Warryn didn't know how to fill. It opened up heart issues that existed long before we met. We, like many couples, maybe thought that our marriage would fix our brokenness, but that's not how it works. It takes a lot of work, not just saying "I do," to get your soul right.

After Warryn told me the truth, I made myself sit down and ask those tough *why* questions. Why had it all unraveled? Why had we ended up in this place? With the benefit of hindsight, I saw the warning signs. When I looked at our emails and text messages, for months they'd all been about business. There were no *I love you*s, nothing personal from either of us. It was all about when we would be in the studio next and plans for Krista's birthday party. And let's not even talk about how there'd been no sex.

I recalled how Warryn had asked me to be home more often, to not travel as much. But I was blind to what he was really asking me. My husband told me that he felt lonely, that he felt left off on the side while I was married to my career, and I basically responded that he had to figure himself out on his own. *Hello, I'm a Grammy Award–winning gospel singer, and you want me to what, sit at home and wash dishes?*

I'm not making excuses, and I'm not owning someone else's behavior or choices. Another person's sin is never your fault. But I want you to understand that letting go involves understanding your own place in the story where you find yourself, and the soul work involves seeing the big picture, not just the pain. No matter how bad things seem, there's always a why, and it's through that discovery that God makes a path to the other side.

As we tried to wade through the mess, there was an afternoon I found myself in our bishop's office with both my husband and the other woman, trying to find some kind of reconciliation. The Bible says that if someone sins against you to bring the situation to "one or two others . . . that every charge may be established by the evidence," and that's what I did. I had the chance to ask questions, to seek the truth, to hear all the sides of the story in front of an authority who would hold us all accountable.

That's something else to understand: in a close relationship, letting go doesn't mean rolling over and accepting anything less than the truth. It doesn't mean letting other people act against you without consequences. This meeting was important because I needed honesty. This meeting would help me decide whether to stay or not.

I kept my cool throughout the conversation. I had decided in advance that I wasn't going to be a person who acted like a fool, trying to get revenge. I wasn't going to get careless just because someone else did.

When I had heard as much as I needed to hear, I told the other woman, "I'm not judging you. Maybe you'll find real love one day. And if you do, I hope no one does to you what you've done to me."

When that was out, I felt the first layer of pain release from my heart, and I knew that this person who had wronged me wasn't going to hold me captive forever. This was not going to be a permanent stain on my life or my marriage. In our wedding vows, I said "for better or worse," and this was definitely worse, but I was still here and I wanted to be free. I wanted to let God use this terrible situation for something good, to grow us all in ways that He saw we needed to grow. And so I prayed right there, "Okay, Lord, I'm done. I want you to take this out of my heart."

I heard His answer. "You can't just let go of your anger. You have to forgive her."

"Come on, really, God?" my heart responded. "Can't I stay just a little mad? Please?"

But no, we can't hold "just a little" back when we do it God's way.

This was tough. That woman had threatened everything important to me. But when God says to forgive, you forgive.

It didn't happen that day, or for a long time, but eventually I walked over to her after a Sunday church service and said the words, "I want you to know I forgive you." I don't know how the words landed on her heart, but I felt free!

Does that mean everything after that was easy? Oh, no. My forgiveness was tried over and over. And it took a long, long time to rebuild trust in my marriage.

The Bible says all things work together for good for those who love God. That's a hard thing to think about, especially when you're in the middle of a mess like I was. For a long time, you could not convince me that what I went through in my marriage would work out for my good. I went to church, and I read my Bible, and I kept singing, but it all felt flat and empty. *This isn't fair, God,* I complained.

And God reminded me that lots of stuff in life isn't fair. He showed me that I'd done plenty of things in my life that demanded forgiveness and understanding from my husband. Wasn't I the one who had been a serial dater? In fact, wasn't I the one who'd been with another guy while Warryn and I were dating? Long before I was in the place to extend forgiveness, I'd had to ask his forgiveness, and even though my cheating was a blow to his self-esteem, he'd offered me grace and mercy.

I stuck with God, and I stuck with my marriage. And day

by day, month by month, I saw God turn my heart and put the pieces back together. He repaired. He restored. He revived. War-ryn and I went to counseling and therapy. We asked a lot of hard *why* questions about our ping-pong match of forgiveness, and how our separate histories of past pains and hurts had brought us here. We got serious about what we really needed from each other, and we fell deeper in love than we'd ever been before. We started to pay attention to each other like never before, and our relationship became not just better, but beautiful. We put God at the center of our relationship. We refused to let the enemy thwart our future or destroy our destiny.

Today, I'm not just married, but I'm happily married. Sure, we've had our issues since then. I've been upset, and he's been upset. We've had the seasons where the fire didn't burn as bright. But when I come through the door at the end of a long day or a long trip, I know that not only are my kids going to rush toward me and scream "Mommy!" but my husband's going to come around the corner with a smile and a "Hey, baby" that says he's glad that I'm home, too. And his smile still makes my heart race. That's better than awards. That's better than screaming fans. Our family is better than ever because we've come through it.

Why am I telling you all of this? Because this is a story that could have destroyed me, but it doesn't own me today. The enemy didn't own me. God showed me how to let go. And not just that, but He gave me a tool that helped my ministry. God knew that one day I would be a first lady and a radio host, some-one who's trusted to hear other people's hardest stories. And no one I've met who's been married for a while has gotten through it without some kind of hard story. It's not always infidelity, but our closest relationships often face attack.

Today, when people come up to me and say, "Oh, you'll never understand what I'm going through. You're famous. I've seen you on TV. You have a great family," I can say, "Girl, pull up a chair and let's talk. I understand more than you think, but I've learned a thing or two about life."

I've had some long years of hard soul work, full of nights when I felt like I was hanging on by a thread. I would sit in the dark and listen to my own music, trying to survive day by day, hoping that I would feel alive again at some point. I would get on stage and cry while I sang, and I'd have to apologize to the audience. "Sorry, guys, it's all real for me tonight. I know you're here, but right now I'm singing to the Father."

That's the thing about being a songwriter who lets God direct me. The Lord has a sense of humor, and sometimes even as I'm writing a song, I think, *Why am I saying this? I know that God's going to give me a story for this song, and I'm going to have to face this. He's going to make sure that I really believe this.*

That was my experience with the song "Forgiven Me," a song that still can make me tear up today.

> *I hold a memory of myself*
> *Reflections of what I used to be*
> *These broken roads that got me here*
> *Can make it hard to face reality*

But a new day is here
It's time that I embrace it
Can't wait another day
Right now I gotta face it

I never ever wanna press rewind
Never wanna go back in time
Not much glory
In that story but it's mine so I'm
Loving who I am today
The past has passed away
Finally I
Have forgiven me

I hold a memory of myself
So young and foolish and not knowing
Careless decisions that I made
I wish somebody would have told me
But a new day is here
It's time that I embrace it
Can't wait another day
Right now I gotta face it

The mirror on the wall
It makes me see today
That I'm, I'm not that foolish girl
Time has brought a change

A transformation
The old into the new
When I let go of me
And held onto you

Has your past passed away? Is there someone you need to forgive? Something you need to let go?

The Bible is pretty clear that forgiveness is not optional. Ephesians 4:32 instructs us, "Be kind to one another, tender-hearted, *forgiving one another*, even as God in Christ forgave you."

But saying that is easier than doing it. Forgiveness is hard. It happens in the heart, and a lot of times you'll have to do it over and over again. You'll say you forgive, but there's still resentment in your heart. You'll think you're over stuff, but then a song or memory will trigger a new round of feelings. You may not even want to do it, because you feel justified in your anger. The enemy likes to tell us that some offenses are unforgivable.

Forgiveness isn't about how bad the thing was that someone else did. It's not about pretending that it didn't matter. It's about closing off those negative feelings that are blocking your future and opening yourself instead to what God is doing inside you. It's about creating the space for Him to work. After all, can you justify asking God to give you something that you're not willing to give yourself?

Holding onto bitterness, holding a grudge, or keeping pain as a pet is like a cancer in your body. I have a friend who has Stage 4 cancer, and before they started treatment the doctor asked, "Is there someone who you're holding anger against? Is there anyone you have not forgiven? Because unforgiveness can take root in your body and make it harder for your cells to heal." And in my friend's case there was someone, and so he needed to work his way down a path of forgiveness before he could turn his energy to fighting the cancer.

A lot of you have lived with the pain and uncomfortable feeling of unforgiveness for a long time. You feel it in your body. It makes it hard to eat. It makes your stomach hurt. It makes you act all out of sorts, yet you dwell on your pain or your anger as a shield.

You're not going to feel good in your body or your soul until you get this right. Until you let go and forgive.

If you want to live a full life—one that is joyful, hopeful, honest, and free—deal with the forgiveness you need to give, with the release that you need to give, and be free. Forgiveness is the only thing that will allow God to restore, repair, renew, and revive the pieces of your heart, to put the pieces of that puzzle back together.

It's the only way that your life will make sense again.

Chapter 7

Surround Yourself

Not long after I became the first lady of our new church, I went to a leadership conference just for women in ministry.

I've always been open about the fact that I had reservations about starting a church. Okay, they were more than reservations. When Warryn first brought it up, I flat-out fought the idea. I felt like I already had a ministry established in my music, and I knew from watching my aunt Theresa serve as a first lady that leading a church was a tough job and put a lot of pressure on a family.

My aunt and uncle poured themselves into their ministry. Their doors were always open. They were always going to the hospital to visit someone or to jail to bail someone out. People were always staying in their house or borrowing their car. I didn't feel equipped to take on that kind of life. That's why I'd married a music producer, not a pastor!

The story of how God brought me around and helped me fall in love with my church is a story for another time. For now, let's just say that when I went to that women's leadership conference, I was still feeling my way through what it meant to be a first lady. I also wasn't sure what to expect from a bunch of other church women.

You know what I'm talking about. Things can get tense when you put a group of women in a room together, even when they're Christians. There are times when instead of really seeing each other, we get competitive. Who's getting the most attention? Who's the prettiest? Who's the most successful? Who's the smartest one? How is my job, my man, my church, or my outfit going to measure up to hers? Those petty issues with "pretty" come up a *lot* when women get together, and sometimes it just feels like too much work to feel out the room—who's nice, who has an agenda, who's soaking up the energy, who needs to be seen?

I've been in rooms of women where the air was so tense you could taste it.

But this particular group of women turned out to be beautiful, and just what I needed. We were a multicultural crowd of first ladies and pastors and ministry directors who all worshipped together and then got honest about our experiences in leadership. I discovered that these women, even the ones who'd been in church ministry for years, all asked the same questions I did. We were all trying to figure out how to protect our families' private lives while also being available for church members who needed us. We all felt pressure to be everything to everyone, have all the answers, and respond to emergencies that we weren't qualified to handle. And at the same time, we all felt incredibly blessed by the opportunity to be involved in bringing people closer to God.

I can't tell you how healing and encouraging it was to laugh that weekend with other women about things that only a church leader would really understand, like how at the end of an amazing service there's always that person who comes up and says something like, "Yeah, that was a great message, but I wanted to let you know that I hate the bathrooms in this building. Can you guys change the color of the paint?"

When you're trying to find your way through life, there's nothing like hearing a person who's farther along the road you're traveling say, "I know exactly what you're talking about. I've been there, too." And when you have questions, or are going through tough times, there's nothing like a group of girlfriends who come alongside you with, "You know what, you're facing something big. We're going to fast and pray with you for three days. Let's get off social media so we aren't distracted and hear from God."

We were created with a need and desire for relationship and community. After God created man, He stopped and said, "It is not good that man should be alone." And in Proverbs 11:14, He reminds us that "in the multitude of counselors there is safety."

When Jesus walked the earth, He gathered twelve disciples. Now, I don't think He did that just because He wanted some guy talk in the evenings after the crowds went home. Every story the Bible records is an example for us about how we should live. Do you really think God was tired on the seventh day of creation? No, because God doesn't get tired. But He gave us an example of how to pause and reflect. In the same way, Jesus' choice to surround Himself with disciples was a way to show us how important friendship, fellowship, and community are.

So even if you think of yourself as an introvert or a loner, God created a piece of your soul to long for love from people who will show you their true selves, so that you can be your true self. Only when you embrace that and open yourself to others will you find the fullness of His plan for you. As Ecclesiastes says, "A threefold cord is not quickly broken." In the middle of counsel, you, too, find safety.

The enemy's strategy has always been to divide us so that we're more vulnerable and easier to deceive, and it's working. The world tells women that our natural state is to be catty, and these days being petty is something we brag about. People today too often act like there's only so much love and attention to go around, and if they want some, that they have to take it from someone else. It's all a competition, pitting one person against another, and leading to a breakdown of life-affirming relationships. Watch the news and you'll hear that there are fewer young people going to church, more broken families, more people moving hundreds or thousands of miles for a job, and more people working so much they don't have time for anything else. We spend more time with our phones than we do in face-to-face conversations, and the internet is teaching us to shout first and ask questions later.

It's time to stop that. It's time to put down our phones and start having real conversations with people we trust, about things that matter.

Up to this point in the book, I've focused on helping you understand and take control of what's happening inside your own heart and mind, and on the relationship you have with God. But now it's time to look outside, at how you're living in the world around you. Your soul work doesn't stop at the edge of your own body.

How you see yourself as a child of God will be influenced by who has influence over you. You need people in your life—and not just any people, but people who bring prayer, wisdom, laughter, love, truth, support, correction, care, and concern to your life.

Who are the people who know you best? If I asked you to make a list of five or ten people who know your heart, and who you trust to listen to you and guide you, could you come up with the names? If I asked who you trust as a spiritual mentor and prayer warrior, could you point to a person in your life who is there to guide you?

You already know that I'm blessed to have a big, close family, but I also have a group of friends who have been with me since we were all kids at church together. Those girls have seen it all—the poor years, the successful years, the failures and fears, the broken engagements, the marriage, the kids, the music, everything. They remember the days when I couldn't give them $2 to pitch in for gas. Once upon a time, we were whispering and giggling together in the back of choir practice, and today we're getting together for lunch to talk about parenting and careers.

We've been through some crazy stuff and plenty of silly stuff.

But what makes us friends isn't just our ability to play together. It's our commitment to hold each other up and hold each other accountable. These were the girls who, in our high school years, made a pact that we'd all protect our purity and stay on "the virgin islands" together. If someone had a date, we'd check in with her after. "How'd it go? Are you still on the island?" Whenever I felt like I was getting "too close" with a boyfriend, one of the things that helped me stay committed to my principles was that I knew I'd have to answer to my G's.

Even today, my girls know my heart and who I am. When Mary Mary first started to take off, these were the friends I relied on to keep me grounded. When one of them said, "You're not going to have time for us anymore now that you're famous," I told her that would never happen. I was still Erica Atkins, and I needed them to help me always remember that. And they have. If any one of them calls me and says, "Too much, E, you're doing too much," I know without a doubt that I've gone off the rails.

As years have passed, I've added new friends to my mix, especially women who are also in ministry and in music. These are the people who commiserate with me when the studio session didn't go well or I'm struggling to find balance in my busy life. Like those women at the ministry conference, they bless me publicly and guide me privately as I move into new seasons of life and new projects.

These are the women I think about when I read what Paul told Philemon, "We have great joy and consolation in your love, because the hearts of the saints have been refreshed by you."

⁓

The thing that ties all of my friends together is that we're grounded in the same truths. We all love Jesus, and we all set out to honor Him first. I can trust these women because I know where they're coming from.

Do your friends help you go in God's directions? Are they people who build you up and encourage you to follow His plan? Loyalty to the wrong people can lead you away from your destiny. Paul wrote in 1 Corinthians 15:33, "Evil company corrupts good habits." And Proverbs 13:20 reminds us that "he who walks with wise men will be wise, but the companion of fools will be destroyed."

When you surround yourself with good people, you are protected. But when you open yourself to the counsel of those who lead you away from God, you'll end up going nowhere. If you're trying to get your life on track and your heart right with God, but you're still spending every Friday night with your girl who always wants to go to the bar and drink too much, or you're still calling your ex when you're lonely, you're letting yourself get pulled in by the distractions of life.

For a long time, I tried to live with the belief that everyone was my friend. I wanted to love everyone, and be loved by them in return. I wanted to trust everybody. It took a few hard knocks before I understood that not everyone I met would be part of my life the way I wanted them to be. Some people would just carelessly rip me to shreds.

You probably know people like that, too. Every time you see

them, they're ready to go on a negative rant about this thing or that person. Someone offended them, or slighted them, or gave them a reason to complain. They're on what's known today as the "petty parade," and they're proud of it.

Don't follow them into this area of temptation. When you get together with your friends, don't knock what someone else is wearing or complain nonstop about your boss or husband. You can be better than that. God calls you to be better than that. "Petty," after all, is just another word for childish, small-minded, and immature. And who really wants to own that label? God tells us to speak in love, and to "let no corrupt word proceed out of your mouth, but what is good for necessary edification."

In our house, we have a rule that we don't bash each other, and we don't bash anyone else. My daughters and nieces know that I won't tolerate them talking about other girls. Yes, I tell them, I saw what she was wearing, but if you can't say something positive, then hush. Focus more on being your best rather than pointing out someone else's wrong. Surround yourself with people who are committed to doing things to make life better, make themselves better, and build others up.

And if someone's not doing that, pray that you find your voice and the confidence to speak up.

One day I got a phone call from some friends who wanted to talk about someone we all knew who had gotten herself in some trouble. "We wanted to make sure you knew about so-and-so. Her situation is so sad, and I just can't believe it. We're all praying for her."

Praying? Oh, I could get behind praying. "Yeah, let's call her," I told them. "Let's pray with her right now." But they didn't want to do that. They really wanted to gossip, and to hide it behind a prayer label. They hung up their phones really quick, and they've never called me to "pray" for anyone again.

If someone in your life starts to go off on a tangent about another person, you have a choice in how you respond. You can let that gossiping spirit fill your heart and jump right in with comments of your own. You can sit by silently and let the negative words continue without contributing to them. Or you can follow the instructions of Ephesians 5:11, which says to "have no fellowship with the unfruitful works of darkness, but rather expose them."

As I said before, you can't force someone else to change. Only God can change someone's heart, so don't get rude or angry. Remember what we said in the last chapter about not letting things get personal. Instead, let the Holy Spirit use your voice to ask, "How is this conversation making us better?" If someone is making a joke at someone else's expense, let them know you don't think it's funny. So what if you didn't like her weave or the way she handled that situation with her kid? So what if she tripped going up on stage? She's doing the best she can. Leave her alone. Let her live her life. It's not always easy to confront someone we love, but the alternative is to let that person keep dragging others down.

If they don't respond to your questions, or notice that you're not laughing with everyone else, consider adding some separation in your relationship. You don't have to expose yourself to someone's poison or put yourself in positions that distract from your purpose. You don't have to say yes every time a person wants to see you. You don't have to answer the phone every time they call. If you're asked about it, be honest without accusing. Say, "I need to focus on my relationship with God right now," or "I'm trying not to spend so much of my time talking about others, and that's what we seem to do when we're together."

It's one thing to be bold and hold others accountable when they act crazy. It's a whole different lesson to learn how to accept a rebuke for yourself. Proverbs 19:20 tells us to "listen to counsel and receive instruction, that you may be wise in your latter days." When you live in community with others, you'll find yourself drawn to places of humility. Honesty is a gift that you can both give and receive, and it's at the core of every Spirit-led relationship.

No one needs the friend who always says, "Oh, of course you should feel that way. Just follow your heart. God understands." Sometimes your heart is being tempted in bad directions. True counselors encourage you, but they also challenge you and charge you. They give you a safe space to cry when you need to, but they also tell you when to stand up and be strong. You need people in your life who can recognize the enemy's attacks and will point you the other way. You need the friends who aren't afraid to say, "That's stupid, don't do that. Don't call him if he's married. Pick up your Bible. Stop going to those places."

Over the years, I've been blessed by some godly people who knew just how to call me back to Jesus. I didn't always hear them well—I've already told you about how my ego got in the way of hearing correction when it came to my career—but there are two moments in my life that have taught me a lot about how to give and receive rebuke.

When I was younger, I led worship in the church where I grew up. One Sunday, I wore a dress to church that I thought was pretty. It was green velvet, sleeveless, and although it wasn't super short, it did show off my legs.

At the end of the service, one of the older women, Sister Emory, came up to me. "That is a beautiful dress," she said. "I can imagine that it's just perfect for a cocktail party or a wedding." And then she smiled at me, and her eyes were nothing but sweet and kind. "But I don't think it's so good for standing in church and leading worship."

I could have been defensive. I could've had a bad attitude. I was the worship leader, after all, and who was she to tell me what to wear? But her words were gentle, and her compliment was sincere, and the Holy Spirit nudged me not to just listen, but to agree with her. She was right. I shouldn't wear that dress to church again, and I never did.

Years later, when I was Erica Campbell and part of Mary Mary, a gospel artist showed me another way to offer truth in love. There had been a series of events happening in the world that fired up my sense of social injustice, and Tina and I announced that until things changed, Mary Mary would not be performing in a certain state. We didn't want to bring the revenue or attention that came with our concerts to a place that we felt was doing more harm than good in urban communities.

Not long after I posted our decision online, I got a message from that artist who was also a pastor and in that area. He understood our reasons for the boycott, he said, but he told me that there were still a lot of people in his region who needed Mary Mary. Yes, there were other artists who could do gospel concerts there, but he reminded me that Tina and I brought something unique to our events. Our concerts often drew people who were unchurched.

"If you don't come," he said, "those people possibly could miss out on experiencing and receiving God's love. So I want to ask you to reconsider your decision."

It was one of the nicest rebukes I've ever gotten, and when I read his message prayerfully, I knew he was right. Tina and I hadn't taken everything into consideration. We changed our policy, and we even went to that pastor's city to sing. We became good friends.

Now, years later, I still occasionally get messages from him when I've gotten worked up about something. "Hey, my sister, can you consider this?" And then he shares with me another perspective. He never challenges me, never tells me directly that I'm wrong or questions my motivations. Like the woman in church who called me on the dress, he always starts by finding our common ground and where we agree. Then, using that, he finds a way to help me see where I should consider another perspective.

If only everyone in the world could offer that kind of grace. God, give me the kind of grace that starts "Hey, my sister, can you consider this?" when someone else is out of line.

There are lots of people who will challenge you over the years, and not all of them will come to you with respect and love. Some of the hardest situations might come from right inside your family.

There's an older woman in our community who I've known for a long time. For as long as I remember, she was mean. She'd see someone in church and say, "Oh, you got so fat!" Or she'd see a cousin or niece at a family event and ask, "What are you doing wrong, honey? Why aren't you married yet?" She would tell parents that their babies were ugly, and asked married couples without children why they were waiting, because they weren't getting younger. It got to the place where people would wince and wait for the insult every time she opened her mouth. Being around her was rough.

Now she's older, and I've heard from her family that they're having trouble caring for her. No one wants to do it, because she didn't plant the seeds of healthy relationships, love, or respect. Now that she needs her family around her, she is reaping what she has sown.

Some of you know just what that family's going through. Family can be tough. Your family may not surround you with prayer and love. You may have lost your parents already, or you may not be physically or emotionally close to them. You may not have grown up in a faith-filled home. Your family may have serious issues with abuse. I've heard all kinds of stories.

As I've gotten older, I'm blessed that my sisters, brothers, and mom are still my closest counsel and best friends. The Atkinses have always been tight. Sure, there were a lot of us, but that meant that we shared more. My mom never let us get away with rivalries or fights. If she came home and two Atkins kids were going at it, she'd break it up. "Stop and hug your sister," she'd demand. At one time or another, I've slept in the same room with at least five of my sisters, and of course Tina and I have been almost inseparable our whole lives.

Our love runs deep, although that might not be obvious at first glance because the counter to my mom's sweetness was always my dad, the master of sarcasm. As kids, we learned to tease each other and challenge each other. Even today, we have zero tolerance for fakeness when we're together. If I call one of my sisters with a problem, it's not because I want compliments and empathy; it's because I know I need some common sense and for someone to tell me the truth.

But here's the thing about the Atkinses: we all love Jesus. We pray together and for each other. We sing in each other's churches. We share the Word of God with each other. Almost every morning, my brother will text us all a Scripture to guide or encourage us through the day.

It's those bonds that carried Tina and me through all of the ups and downs of Mary Mary, and then all of the uncertainty when we decided to pursue solo projects. Tina was in the front row for me when I released *Help*, and I was in the front row for her when her solo album, *It's Personal*, came out. We sing backup on each other's songs, we collaborate in our writing, and we talk all the time, about everything.

Are we perfect? Of course not. Do I agree with every decision that every one of my family members makes? Of course not. But whatever happens, I know that they're always going to be there for me. They surround me and protect me, just like a good family should.

If you have a family member who never sowed the right seeds with you, that's not a person who you need to constantly invite to dinner. If that person is in a place with you and things go south, stand up and be kind, but get in your car and go home. Pray for your family member and wish them well, but keep a distance. You don't have to have Thanksgiving dinner with people if all it will do is stir up trouble.

But if it's in your power to sow healthy seeds and the Holy Spirit opens the door, don't let your family relationships slide away. "A brother is born to help in time of need," says Proverbs 17:17 (NLT). The enemy works overtime to break up families, and sometimes a dispute or difference can be worked through. New seeds can be sown. After all, your family is your first line of defense and the people who will be with you through thick and thin. It may be time to repent of your own ego and put aside those squabbles about who crashed your car, or who broke the bicycle, and get to know one another as adults.

Knowing when to build bridges and when to set boundaries isn't easy, but God gave me a prayer to guide me through it.

When I became a solo artist, one of my first challenges was assembling the team who would help me release my debut album. Warryn was still my producer, of course, but we had to hire people to manage the release, schedule the tour, handle the press, build relationships with radio, and generally keep the project on track. Some had worked with Mary Mary, and some knew Warryn, and some were new to me.

For the first time in my career, my team just didn't work. They were all great people individually, but they just couldn't seem to get fully on board together. They were distracted by conflicts, with everyone complaining about what someone else wasn't doing. It seemed like nothing was right or on time.

With the release date approaching, I was totally stressed. I couldn't make these people get along! And so I did what I should have done in the first place: I turned it over to God and asked Him to *reveal* to me what needed to happen. If there was something that I could do to *repair* the situation, I would. But if not, I prayed that God would *remove* the people who were causing the block and *replace* them with people who were ready to go.

God was listening.

Two weeks before the release, three of the team members quit. That almost never happens in the music industry. An album release is a huge undertaking, and with two weeks left, everyone should be in go mode. There are schedules to finalize for tours and media, radio and digital to coordinate, press releases and images to prep, everything. But God had heard my prayer, and He knew that while it would be hard to work without them, it would have been so much harder to keep trying to work with them.

It was a powerful reminder about release. In Judges 7, God's servant Gideon was about to go into battle against the Midianites. With thirty-two thousand men lined up behind him, he was probably feeling pretty good about his chances. But God said no. "The people who are with you are too many for Me to give the Midianites into their hands, lest Israel claim glory for itself against Me, saying, 'My own hand has saved me.'" He told Gideon to release any of his soldiers who were afraid, and twenty-two thousand left.

Gideon was down to just ten thousand soldiers, but God said he still had too many. There was a second test, where the men went down to the water to drink. God told Gideon to release every man who let down his guard and got down on his knees to drink directly from the water. Only the men who kept their eyes up and drank from cupped hands, "as a dog laps," should remain.

In the end, Gideon had only three hundred men to take on an army that the Bible says were "lying in the valley as numerous as locusts; and their camels were without number, as the sand by the seashore in multitude."

Why would God do that? Because He wanted to make it clear that when Gideon's army defeated their enemy—and with God's help, they did—it was He who won the battle, not the Israelites. If they'd had all of their soldiers and all of their resources, then they could take the credit. But when God limited them, they had to acknowledge Him.

That's what happened to me with the album release. I'd put together a top-tier team and a big strategy. These people had taken many artists before me to the number-one spot. Team EC looked unstoppable, until God said no. He tied my hands behind my back and reminded me that as important as it was to have people, it was more important to have Him. And with Him, *Help* released on time, hit the Billboard Top Ten, and stayed #1 on the Gospel chart for seven weeks.

God can restore any broken relationship, but He doesn't always choose to do it, or do it right away. Sometimes it takes years. Sometimes it never happens. If you have a lot of people in your life or your church or your business, but you're not sure they're the right people, you can use this prayer asking God to Reveal, Repair, Remove, and Replace:

God, reveal to me whether I am surrounding myself with the people You want. If I am, show me how to repair what is broken. If not, please remove them and replace them with the people You choose.

If something feels damaged, don't try to fix what can't be fixed. Go back to that *why* question and let God show you the reasons that things are off. If someone's heart isn't right, or if the other person doesn't desire a healthy relationship, then back away. Let God remove the people who aren't right and replace them with what He wants for you. You've done your part.

Only God can bring you the right people. You can go to church, you can be generous, and you can serve in ministry, but in the end, He will show you who you need and when you need them.

If someone leaves, wish that person well and let them go. That person wasn't for you in this season of your life. God's got a better plan, a bigger plan, and they're not part of it.

So where do you find those people who are wise, who are supportive, and who bring joy to your life? They might be in your neighborhood, in your workplace, or in your workout group. But for me, there's never been a better place to find true friends and mentors than a solid, Bible-teaching, community-affirming, Jesus-loving church.

No matter how unstable our living situation was, my parents always made sure that the Atkins family was in church on Sunday morning. God was our constant, and being connected to the body of believers was our source of strength. Both of my parents served in the church, and so everyone there knew us—and at times when I was a kid, it seemed like everyone was watching us. The press and gossip bloggers today have nothing on the elders of my childhood church. Anytime one of us did something wrong, we heard, "I'm going to tell your dad," or "Where's Sister

Atkins?" We learned quick how to conduct ourselves, wherever we were.

But we also learned that we could depend on our church family. My church was full of love—for each other, for God, and for our community. As a choir member and lead singer, it was the center of my world. My best friends grew up with me there. My pastors and leaders gave me sound biblical and life advice when I needed to make tough decisions, and the older women became mentors and guides. We prayed, we sang, we laughed, and we listened to each other. We were a family and still are. I found joy there that lasts to this day.

Does that mean I liked all of them all the time, and we always got along? Of course not. You can't bring a group of people together and expect that everyone will have personalities that match. I spent my share of time sitting in the back pew, mad about one thing or another. But I always found my way back to the choir stand.

Church isn't supposed to be easy. It's not supposed to make you feel pampered and coddled. A church is like a family or a group of friends; it's work. Brother So-and-So is going to say something that you disagree with, and Sister So-and-So is going to hurt your feelings. The pastor's going to say something that convicts your heart and leaves you in tears.

The truth does not always feel good, but the truth is what will help you grow. One of the blessings of a church is the way it teaches you to respect and work with people to whom you wouldn't normally find a connection. Because in the end, the important thing is that you know you're all going in the same direction.

In Matthew 18:20, Jesus reminds us that "where two or three are gathered together in My name, I am there in the midst of them." And Hebrews 10:25 reminds us to "not [forsake] the assembling of ourselves together."

When you're part of a church that teaches truth, that challenges you to live a Christ-centered life, and that loves and cares for its community, you're in a great place to grow. Those flawed, imperfect, growing believers may make you crazy, but they'll protect you from the real enemy—the one who wants to kill, steal, and destroy you. Even if that enemy shows up in church, that's not a reason not to go.

On the other hand, I'm not telling you that you have to go to church a certain number of times per week, or that you can't find your tribe of Christian friends somewhere else. I don't think church works very well when people feel pressured to be there.

If you're in tune with the Holy Spirit and listening to His guidance, then you'll know whether He wants you to be at a service on Saturday night, or whether you should set aside some private date time for your husband instead. Maybe your kids need a day with their mom at the park. But sometimes, especially when your spirit is dry, the Lord will draw you toward the place where the stream of His life and energy flows most freely. If you are seeking Him, He will make an indentation in the sand that will lead you to the right place and the right people. He'll carve out the road for you.

And as you build relationships with His people, you'll find yourself looking at the calendar and thinking that you can't wait to hear what the Lord has to say today. You can't wait to worship. You can't wait to serve alongside these friends. You can't wait to hear what they have to share with you.

That brings us to the last thing I want to say on this subject in terms of how you surround yourself. Your people are important. They're part of God's plan for you. But they're not God.

For a long time in my life, it was important to me that everyone I respected and loved had a say in my life. When it came to my life decisions, I wanted to know, how did my mom feel? How did my aunt Theresa feel? How did my dad and my pastor feel? How about my friends and my sisters? If anything came up, I would call everyone I knew to get their opinions. *Were we all cool with my direction? Am I doing the right thing?* It was almost an addiction.

I trusted the opinions and spiritual wisdom of other people in my life more than I trusted my own. I went to faithful, prayerful people who always directed me to God and told me to pray, but still, I went to them first. I believed somehow that they would hear God more clearly than I could. My mom and my pastor had been saved longer than me, my mind whispered. God would hear them before He heard me.

But then there was a night when I felt like I was falling apart, and no one answered their phones. I mean really, no one. I went down my whole list. I had a decision to make, and I was sitting in my car in the middle of the night, and for the first time in my life, not a single person was there to talk to me.

For a moment, I lashed out at God. _Really, Lord? You're going to put me in a mess and then leave me all by myself to deal with it?_

And I heard the Holy Spirit answer me. _Hello? Who says you're alone? Isn't it Me and you? Or is it them and you? Who is first in your life?_

I remembered again that favorite passage in Proverbs 3:5–6: "Trust in the Lord with all your heart, and lean not on your own understanding." It was like God was waving a flag and saying, "Trust in Me. Ask Me first, and I will guide you. I'll show you the way to go. You are strong enough on your own to hear Me. You have done the soul work to find Me. I am here."

And so, even though this is a chapter where I want you to see the importance of creating a community of support, I also want you to remember this:

Other people come second to God. When you are in tune with the Holy Spirit, He will reveal to you directly what you need and who you need, and He will provide them, because He is always the center. Trust Him before you talk to them.

Chapter 8

Take Care of Yourself

If there's anything you've learned from this book so far, I hope it's that you are more than your exterior. Your beauty goes so much deeper than what you see in a photo. How you live, how you serve, and how you love are more important than the size of your dress or the shape of your nose.

But don't get too carried away with that idea or think that this book somehow gives you permission to ignore your body. Doing your soul work is not an excuse to think what you do with your body doesn't matter.

I know moms whose meals are always the kids' leftover French fries and chicken nuggets, and professionals whose only exercise is walking from their desks to their refrigerators. I know single women who think that they have to use their bodies as the lure to find a man, and wives who stop making an effort because they already have a man.

None of that is part of God's plan.

God didn't just give you a soul; He also gave you a body. And there's no way for you to take care of the inside without also taking care of the outside. There's no way to fully love yourself and never wash your face or comb your hair in the morning. So this is the chapter where we talk about bodies that are "fearfully and wonderfully made," because your soul work includes your choice to honor and respect everything God gave you.

I know how hard it can be, as a woman, to keep up with the fast pace of your life, and how easy it is to sacrifice your own health so you can take care of everyone else.

Right after my son Warryn III was born, my schedule was crazy. Mary Mary had just released our fifth album, and we were touring the country and doing all kinds of media while I was also nursing a new baby and taking care of a toddler. I wasn't sleeping right, and I wasn't eating right. Then one night, just as Tina and I walked off the stage from a performance at the Dove Awards, my vision got blurry and I felt a sharp pain in the back of my neck. I could barely walk. I had never felt like that before. Usually, if something starts to hurt, I try to sleep it off, but this was totally different.

"I've got to go to the hospital right now," I told Warryn, and we skipped the rest of the show and went straight to the ER. The doctors there discovered that my blood pressure was through the roof. I was on the verge of a stroke. They put me on high blood pressure medication and gave me a lot of rules about eating better, resting more, and losing some weight.

It was a scary night, but I didn't take the bigger picture seriously enough at first. I didn't think that people like me—in my thirties, active, and not that fat—could have health problems like that. So instead of getting with the program, I complained about picking up a prescription. I changed my diet a little and lost some more of the baby weight, and then decided that everything was fine. I stopped taking the medicine and slipped back into old habits.

But the next time I went to see my doctor, my blood pressure was up again. This time the doctor sat me down and explained in no uncertain terms that I was stressing out my heart muscle by making it work so hard, and if I kept it up, I could do irreparable damage.

That was the wake-up call I needed to make my health a priority. I went back to taking the medicine. I started exercising regularly. I paid more attention to what I ate. I even gave up Cheetos, and I love Cheetos.

But I love God more than Cheetos, and I knew that He'd given me not just a body, but a "temple of the Holy Spirit who is in you," as it says in 1 Corinthians 6:19. Paul makes it clear that "you are not your own." When I mistreated or neglected myself, what I was really doing was mistreating or neglecting the image of God. I was letting His temple get dirty.

Your temple doesn't come with replacement parts. If you don't take care of yourself, you can't just go to the lung store or the kidney store to get a new one. If you eat badly or drink yourself into a stupor or don't take care of your skin or don't honor your sexuality, there will be consequences that will follow you for the rest of your life.

Scripture tells us in Romans to "present your bodies a living sacrifice, holy, acceptable to God, which is your reasonable service." What does your sacrifice look like? Are you giving God a temple that's all beaten and misused? Are you like the dented can or box in the grocery store? "Oh, you know, the bread itself is fine, but the packaging is just a little torn." Or are you cultivating and caring for the reflection of God that He's put in your care?

Now, some of you have health issues that you were born with, or that you've been carrying for years, and I'm not talking about how you live with those. If you're living the best you can with the body you have, you're a good caretaker of your temple. What matters here isn't your physical capacity, but the way that you're treating what you've been given.

I'm talking about the choices you make every day to abuse or respect yourself. I'm talking about the junk food and chemicals that fuel us, the drugs and alcohol that medicate us, the chair that we never get up from, the screen that we never turn off, the men we can't quite turn away from. Every one of them leaves a little dent in the packaging God gave you.

No matter how strong the temptations might be, you do not need to give in to your body's physical cravings, whether they're for food or sex or attention or whatever. God blessed you with a mind that is capable of self-control, and He tells you to use it. He gives you the power to do the work to develop discipline with the help of the Holy Spirit inside you.

If you feel like your spirit is all over the place and your mind is distracted by every little thing that comes along, take that as a sign that it's time to change, time to fast and pray. If you're past the place where you can do things in moderation, find a way to come full stop for a while to remove the distraction—food or social media or TV or whatever—and give that time and energy entirely to God.

That kind of focus and intention leads to the "renewing of your mind," as it says in Romans 12:2. I love that almost every version of the Bible uses the word *renewing* here, an action word for repetition. Life changes don't happen overnight. Willpower takes time. But you can discipline yourself to make the right choices. It's all an issue of discipline and knowing when to say no. Yeah, your body wants ice cream at noon. It wants that burger and fries. It wants that drink. It wants to watch just one more episode of *This Is Us*. It wants that handsome man's touch.

If you listen to the Holy Spirit, you'll know the consequences before you act—and every action has a consequence. Eat too much of the wrong kinds of food, and you'll add pounds and lose strength. You won't have the energy that you need. Don't get enough sleep, and it will be hard to focus or keep up tomorrow. And as for sex, well, we'll talk about that in a minute. But God does not give you any temptation that you cannot overcome.

Now, did you notice that when I talked about being healthy, I didn't mention once what you weigh?

The world wants you to think that beauty begins and ends with a number on a scale and the size on a tag, and women today, including me, have bought into it wholeheartedly. I've always had curves, and over the years I've tried every gimmick on the planet to keep them in line: SlimFast, SlimSlow, Atkins, lemonade diet, you name it. I've tried more water, all carbs, no carbs, all protein, off sugar, off salt. I've done it all.

I've also talked to a lot of other women about how they feel about their size, and what the number on a scale symbolizes to them. I've known women with eating disorders who are sure they're not small enough, and women whose bodies are breaking down because the weight on their frame is too much to carry. Women cry and break down because they've spent years trying to change their shape, and nothing worked.

If you find yourself worrying and regretting and fretting about your weight, here's the thing to remember: God doesn't see you as a number. Part of the soul work of honoring your body is shifting this conversation away from your size and toward the place where you can live in your truth as the healthiest version of yourself that you can be, whatever that looks like for you.

I love the movement that's happening now in the entertainment industry, as we learn to develop an appreciation for people of all sizes. I'm grateful for the women who stand up and show the world that they're comfortable in their skin, however much of it they have. Thank God for women like my sister Goo Goo, who is full figured and sassy and downright gorgeous. She's a bold and smart stylist, but it's her confidence that makes her look good in everything she wears. Seriously, everything!

If your weight is controlling your life, and your emotions are all tangled up in what you eat, bring that to the Holy Spirit and let Him redirect your attention. Your stomach should never be your boss. The scale should never be an addiction. Being thin for the sake of being thin is missing the point. Food is God's gift, fuel for the amazing life that He has for you, but it's not your purpose.

God looks at your heart and your intent. Maybe you're in your fifties and aren't the size that you were thirty years ago. Maybe you're in your twenties and aren't the size of your girlfriends. If you're taking care of yourself, physically and spiritually, you're good. If that means you can walk around the block for thirty minutes a day, that's great. And if you're a gym rat working out and polishing your temple two hours a day, God bless you, sister.

I was pretty when I was 118 pounds and living for God, and I was pretty when I was 182 pounds and focused on Him. What matters isn't my number; it's how I feel inside that number. Do I have the energy to get through my busy day? Can I move around on a stage for a concert, stay focused during the meetings, make it across the airport to catch my flight, and still have the energy when I get home to be a good wife and mom? Do I have the health and the focus to listen and follow where God leads? If the answer is yes, then I'm the right size.

Size is only one of the ways we judge our outsides, though. Because whatever you look like, there's probably a deeper human instinct at work, and it has a question:

Am I sexy?

There, I said it. You know we can't spend a whole book talking about being pretty without talking about sexuality. So this is that chapter, too.

But first, let's get something clear: when we talk about being sexy, we're not necessarily talking about having sex. We'll get to the sex in a little bit, but first, I want to have some straight talk about that inner desire you have to be desired.

Most Christians know sex is the thing that married couples are blessed to do and unmarried people are not supposed to do, and then we just leave it there. Whole generations of kids grew up in churches knowing that it was wrong to have sex outside marriage, but not knowing much about how God created human bodies to be drawn toward each other. No one talks about the need for companionship or physical touch.

When I was organizing that first More Than Pretty conference a few years ago, I wanted to find a Christian sex therapist who could help us understand God's perspective on the body, and the chemical and spiritual things that happen within the union of man and woman. I wanted someone to help us get past the idea that sex is something dirty, and show married women how to enjoy both love and lust, and find satisfaction in their physical relationships. But I couldn't find anyone with those credentials. This just isn't something we talk about as believers, and we should.

As women, we've got to find ways to be honest so that our sisters and daughters can stop hiding feelings that they think are wrong. We're leaving them to believe that their human attractions and needs are nasty. And in response, they're running away from God, leaving church, tying themselves to the wrong guys or girls, and winding up pregnant or having abortions, all because no one wants to teach or talk with them honestly about sexuality.

The enemy wants you to feel either unable to control your desires or ashamed for your natural human instincts. He wants to break your sexiness apart from your spiritual life. But that's a lie.

Here's the truth: God gave men and women hormones that draw us to each other. We all want, instinctively, to be attractive to other people, to draw and hold their attention. And sexual energy—sexiness—is one of the ways we get there. When it's used for God's purposes within marriage, sexiness creates a bond between two people that can withstand time and trial.

Sure, if you let your sexy get carried away and let it control you, it will lead you into things and places your true spirit is not prepared to go. Just like your stomach should not be your boss, sexiness or lust should not be your boss, either. But the desire itself is not bad. God gave me my curves and the skin that I'm in. He made my body desire connections with others. He wants me to be attractive to my husband, and to find him attractive in return.

When Warryn and I were dating, I dropped into the studio one day to visit him. He was working with a young artist, and I noticed right away that she was just tickled by everything he said. Then I noticed that my boyfriend was telling a lot of jokes. I mean, *a lot* of jokes. The artist was laughing at every single one of them, even the corny ones that weren't all that funny.

The more she laughed, the more jokes he made. Now, I'm not trying to put the guy on blast. Warryn wasn't doing anything wrong. He wasn't trying to push up on this girl, and I was right there in the room. He was just reacting to the attention that he was receiving. A woman was captivated by him, and he was responding to it. That's human nature, appreciating being appreciated. That's what sexiness is.

Some women try to seek out the sexy with their choice of clothes. They mistakenly think that the less fabric they wear, the more they will be admired and desired. I know some uber-sexy virgins who are letting their desire to be desired lead them into all sorts of dangerous territory.

Some women go further and offer sex itself. But that's not the way it works. If you're showing yourself to everyone, hoping someone will pay attention, you're gonna inspire a lot of lust, but that doesn't lead to real appreciation and love.

It's not just women, either. Men also experience this desire to be admired, and some of them try to use their sexy to get that attention. It's what drives them to show off when a woman's in the room or post pictures of themselves showing the beautiful skin God gave them. They want to be seen and appreciated just as much as we do. They want to feel special. (A note about that showing skin, though: if you're standing in your dirty bathroom that you've never cleaned and thinking about taking a selfie in the mirror, put down the phone. No one appreciates that.)

The desire to be seen and admired is what keeps a lot of women in bad relationships. You probably know someone whose boyfriend or husband is just terrible, but she keeps going back because she doesn't want to be alone. Instead of realizing that she's beautiful and necessary, and that she can find peace and contentment as a single woman, she believes she has to put up with all kinds of disrespect. That's what happens when our desire to be desired goes off the rails.

The problem isn't being sexy or sexual. The problem is letting that part of you overpower the rest and lead you into bad decisions.

God created sex, plain and simple. It was His idea that "the two shall become one." My uncle, the pastor of the church where I grew up, used to say, from the pulpit, that if God made anything better than sex, He left it in heaven.

But like most of His gifts to us, it can be misused. There's a reason that the Bible condemns fornication (the fancy word for sex between people not married to one another) more than a dozen times. It's the most personal, intimate act that you can do with your body—with God's temple. The other things that the Bible condemns, like lying and stealing, happen outside the body, but sex happens inside the temple.

"Now the body is not for sexual immorality but for the Lord, and the Lord for the body," Paul says in 1 Corinthians 6:13. And then a few verses later, he continues, "Flee sexual immorality.

Every sin that a man does is outside the body, but he who commits sexual immorality sins against his own body."

We talked earlier about how the Holy Spirit dwells in believers. When you open your body through sex, you bring that act inside you, as well. So where does the Spirit go when you're coming together with someone? If you're acting outside a union that He blessed, where does that leave Him?

Sex is intimate and spiritual, and always involves emotions. You can't just blow off your actions as "friends with benefits" or "hooking up." There's no such thing as casual sex. When a woman has sex with a man, she receives a part of that man. She becomes physically and spiritually connected.

The reason that the Bible is so clear that fornication is a sin isn't because God wants to keep something wonderful from you. It's not because He wants to punish you for being single. It's because sex is such an intimate act, and the impact of it is so great that it has to be protected.

Sure, you can protect yourself from pregnancy and most diseases, but you can't protect yourself from the emotional effects of a broken heart, or pieces of your body that stay with all your sexual experiences.

I wish I could tell you that I was a virgin when I married Warryn, but that would be a lie. I wasn't. I wasn't promiscuous, but I was a girl who loved love, and I made mistakes. I got carried away, and there were consequences. I brought my past experiences into my marriage, and so did Warryn, and we had to work through that as a couple.

That's the thing about sex. It's always there with you. When you finally find the person you want to spend your life with, you carry all of that history with you. If you were in love with Tony when you were nineteen, and you slept with him and he blew your mind, then Tony could still be with you at thirty or fifty, and so is whoever else came along, especially if you didn't get them out of your system, if you didn't break the soul tie. That's a lot of comparison for a husband to live up to. (And if he's slept around, some part of you will always wonder how you measure up.)

You can't erase those connections once they're made, or predict how they will change your perspective later in life.

But Erica, I'm getting older, and I'm still single. I can't keep holding out forever.

Actually, I think you can.

The same Scripture that says "make no provision for the flesh" also promises, in 1 Corinthians 10:13 (NLT), that "the temptations in your life are no different from what others experience. And God is faithful. He will not allow the temptation to be more than you can stand. When you are tempted, he will show you a way out so that you can endure."

There's always a way of escape. God's servant Joseph had to literally run out of a room when his boss's wife came after him for sex. She grabbed his clothes, and he had to slide out of his coat and run. It wasn't easy, but God gave him the way to protect himself.

Many years ago, I went out with an older guy who I liked a lot. We had a good time, and at the end of the evening he suggested we stop at his house. My heart started racing, but I wanted to be cool so I said okay. One thing led to another, and I ended up locked in his bathroom, crying, asking him to just take me home. I was furious with myself for being in the situation, and ashamed that I'd been so overconfident in myself. I learned not to pretend that I was stronger than I was, or that I wasn't vulnerable to a man's touch or embrace. I got better at setting boundaries early.

When Warryn and I were dating, we lived about forty-five minutes away from each other. He would drive all the way across the city to visit me, or I would drive my beat-up car all the way out to see him. When I could, I took Tina with me, so that I had someone for accountability. But there were some times when I knew we would be alone. And it was on those days that I had to repeat, over and over, the Scripture to "make no provision for the flesh."

If he was coming to my place, I had to be conscious to blow out the candles. I had to check my playlist to make sure it wasn't setting the wrong mood. Then I would catch myself thinking about what I was wearing under my clothes and have to stop. *No, Erica, what are you doing? No one's going to see that. Wear your ugliest underwear, the ones with the holes. Turn on your loudest Christian music.* If Tina was out of town, I'd invite my little sisters to come hang out. I'd make sure anybody could come through that door at any time.

Today, when I talk to young women about their dating, it seems not much has changed. If he's coming over to watch Netflix, are they conscious of what movie they're choosing? Don't cuddle up with *Love Jones* or *The Notebook*. Don't pick something that's going to make you misty-eyed and lean into him. Guard yourself.

Sin will always take you farther than you want to go and keep you longer than you want to stay.

You might think that you're making yourself more attractive to a future husband by being available for whatever he wants, but the truth is that he shouldn't be pushing on you for that. You both should be trying to abstain. Guys may take advantage of something they can get for free on Tuesdays, but they're not going to treat you as someone special if you don't treat yourself as someone special. Take your temple seriously, find a guy who loves God and finds his identity in Christ, and let God handle the rest.

And that's the important part: you're too special to set yourself up with some guy who's impatient. If you see the worthiness of yourself in God's eyes, then you need a man who also sees himself and you as worthy of the wait. If you want someone who sees your heart, make sure you're also taking time to look at his. How does he deal with pressure? How does he treat his family? Does he pray? Does he go to church? Does he have a strong work ethic? Does he treat the people around him—not just you, because he's trying to impress you, but his friends and coworkers—with respect?

Don't get swayed by some fine guy's looks or economic status. Don't get swept off your feet by the first brother who makes you laugh. Physical attraction fades, and chemistry can explode.

❧

I know that my experience is not everybody's truth. Some of you grew up in houses where your mom gave you birth control pills at fourteen and your dad had a jar of condoms for your brothers to use whenever they wanted. By the time you picked up this book, you may have had plenty of experience. Sex has always been presented to you as no big deal. I've even met Christians who argue that God doesn't want us to have to wait for marriage anymore, and that the blessing of sex should be open to everyone.

But what I'm saying isn't just my opinion. It's God's command. Hebrews 13:4 (NLT) says, "Give honor to marriage, and remain faithful to one another in marriage. God will surely judge people who are immoral and those who commit adultery."

If you've gone down that road, you can come back. It's never too late to take a broom to your temple and replace the locks on the doors. If you still have soul ties to the past, the Holy Spirit can help you sever and burn them if you ask Him. There is nothing you've done that God can't forgive, and nothing that will keep you from living in His grace and blessing.

Yeah, it's hard to close that door once it's opened. I know a lot of people, men and women, who chose to be celibate as adults. It takes work, but it is possible. Just as minds can be renewed, so can bodies. The key is to surround yourself with supportive friends who will hold you accountable, guard your mind, and stick to your boundaries. Take the focus off the flesh and fill the spaces in your life with more of God, more service, and more of the things that bring you close to Him. Remember, your body is not the boss.

If you're married already as you're reading this, you've already discovered the beauty that comes from experiencing sex within a lifetime union. Marriage is your chance to embrace your sexy and to make it special.

But it's not always that easy. When Christian women spend their whole lives hearing that sex is a sin, they can't just flip the switch overnight. My mother tells the story of how she stood in the bathroom on her wedding night, scared and ashamed, tugging at her negligee and trying to talk herself into going to the other room to be free with her husband. She wasn't ready to embrace the thing that had been forbidden for so long.

Today, I know some women who tried to counter those negative messages from their churches by going outside it to learn the things they didn't know. I know church women who turned to pornography to get their information, and girlfriends who organized trips to the strip club before their sisters got married. But that's not solving anything. A random stranger who doesn't love God and doesn't understand the emotional and spiritual impact of a true connection isn't going to show you the stuff you need to know for a healthy union. You might have learned the act of sex, but the glorious beauty is just as mysterious as it always was.

Some women figure it out, but a lot of wives spend years, even decades, just putting up with sex because it's part of their marriage vows. They see it as something they have to do, but they've never given themselves permission to really desire their husbands or enjoy sex. They still feel like sex is dirty. They've never found the fire, or else they've let it slip away. In the middle of jobs and kids and responsibilities, they've forgotten how to embrace their sexy.

If this is you, I'm here to tell you that you're missing out. That's not how God wants us to be married.

When Warryn and I first got married, we had a lot to learn. We'd had a beautiful, lavish wedding, with five hundred guests and thirteen bridesmaids and groomsmen, four ushers, and three flower girls. We had a theme for the decorations and a reception at a mansion. The whole thing was even featured on a TV show called *A Wedding Story*. It was amazing, like a fairy tale, but once it was over, we didn't know how to be married. We didn't know how to communicate.

He would come home at the end of the day, and I'd be upstairs, ready and waiting for him. But he wouldn't know that. I'd hear him go right to his video games.

Later, when he did come upstairs, I would have lost that loving feeling. *Don't put your toe on my side of the bed, sir. You didn't talk to me all day. You didn't send me a cute text message. You didn't ask me how I was. I don't know if you thought about me at all, but you had time for video games? That's not how this works.*

It took a while for us to learn that if you want a sexy, passionate, fulfilling marriage in the physical sense, you both have to communicate your needs.

This is what I want. This is what I need. How can we make that happen?

Life isn't like the movies. People don't just read your mind. So talk about what you're looking for in terms of affection and attention, face your insecurities and old comparisons, and trust each other enough to be honest. If this is the person you can talk to about your kids and your retirement plans and your credit card bills, you should surely be able to talk about your intimacy and your connectedness.

What do you need to feel loved and intimate? Is it a back rub or some kind of physical touch? Do you need him to talk to you, to tell you in words or notes how he's feeling? Do you need flowers and candles, or just twenty minutes of time to yourself to shift gears after a busy day?

And what does he need? Men and women both enjoy sex. But how does he show you when he needs your physical attention without running the risk of being rejected? It's hard for any man to hear no too often.

I'll tell you this. After eighteen years of experiments, my husband and I have a calendar so that we know when we're both busy and focused on work, the times when I have set aside to get my mind right, and the times when my body is ready and open to him. And when it's *those* times, we make a point to connect.

Because our life involves so much travel, that might mean that one of us gets on an airplane to go where the other one is for a date night. Our time together is that important to us.

Yes, there are nights when we're not going to feel sexy. We're not in the mood for candles, romantic dinners, and sweet whispers. We've both worked hard and have a lot going on, and all we want to do is curl up in our sweats with the remote and watch TV. We're not always feeling all googly-eyed just to be together, but as long as we're still laughing at each other's jokes, that's still appreciation and desire. And you know what? Flirting with my man is so much fun. It's sexy to say things to each other no one else hears and do things no one but he and I know about.

Once you get busy with life, it's possible that your marriage will have a season where the thrill is gone. There doesn't have to be a crisis in your relationship to let distractions get in the way of intimacy and connection. If you start to notice that's happening, don't panic. It's not a sign that your relationship is doomed, and it's something that you can work through and past.

I'm really busy now. I have not just the music, but an entertainment company and a creative ministry, and I have to travel all the time for my radio show. Warryn has a label with a bunch of artists with needs and a church to run. It's really easy for us to come home just to change clothes and then go back out into the world.

Those seasons happen, but the important thing is to be

aware of them and to address them together. We're careful not to treat our house like the place we merely eat and sleep. We're intentional about keeping the excitement of going home to see our mate.

If something seems off in your relationship, talk about it. Cancel a meeting or hire a babysitter and make time to connect with your husband intentionally and on purpose.

Don't start taking his presence for granted. Don't get complacent and think that there's no reason to think about your appearance or how you carry yourself. Whether you've been married for five years or fifty, your husband still wants you to make an effort. I want my husband to be a well-kept man, to take care of himself and to pay attention, and so I give to him what I want him to give to me in return. I get a pedicure before I put that toe over onto his side of the bed. I pay a little attention to my hair.

This is especially important after you have kids, by the way. I know a lot of moms who turn their kids into their idols. I did it at first, when Krista was born. Everything was about her: what she ate, when she slept, what she wanted, how I could serve her. I carried photos of her with me every time I traveled and spread them across the room.

Babies are adorable and needy, and they can't hurt or offend us like adults. (Teenagers, on the other hand, are a different story, but that's for another book!) Little kids love us unconditionally, but where does that leave your husband? I've seen too many situations where Husband becomes Dad, and Dad becomes a servant. He's no longer the head of the house or king of the castle. Instead, he's there to do the chores and pay the bills. He's not an equal or trusted parent, and he doesn't get much personal attention. *Sexy? What's that?*

Warryn is a great dad, but he's also really good at reminding me that he's a husband first, and I am his wife. There was one day in particular when he picked me up at the airport after a trip. Instead of going straight home, he started driving around while we talked, and then he said he wanted to go out to eat.

"Can't we just go home? We'll still be together if we're with the kids," I told him.

He shook his head. "Not yet. You're my girlfriend before you're their mom. I had you first, and once they're grown and leave the house, I'll still be there. We make sure we're good with us first, and then we can bring them in."

So that's what we do, and that's what I encourage you to do in your marriage, as well. Give yourself time to be your husband's girlfriend. Don't talk about cleaning the gutters, or finding a new mechanic, or what the teacher said. Just spend time together having fun, whatever that looks like for the two of you, and see what kind of intimacy is born from that.

Before we finish, I want to say one more thing about your sexy. Because a woman is gifted with curves and soft skin, and a man is gifted with instincts that seek women out, the way you act and the way you carry yourself is going to affect more than just the man you're dating or the man you marry. Whether you're single or married, be aware of how you live your life at work, at church, and when you're just racing through the grocery store.

Are you presenting yourself as a lady?

That might seem like an old-fashioned word, but the world needs more ladies today than ever. A lady—a real lady, not a girl—knows that she is someone to be valued and respected, and she lives her life in a way that draws value and respect.

When you leave your house, how are you dressed? I don't mean do you have new clothes and a face of makeup on, but are you clean? Are you wearing things that fit or are you sloppy?

I had a friend whose first job, many years ago, was at a movie theater. She was always on time and did a good job, but the clothes she wore to work were always wrinkled and dirty. "You're going to lose your job because of that shirt," I warned her. "Girl, go get yourself an iron and look like you care." But she argued that she worked in a dark theater and no one ever saw her or paid attention to her anyway, so why should she bother. A few weeks later, she was fired for being unprofessional.

Are you protecting your temple?

When I first started traveling as a musician, one of the women in my church pulled me aside. "Erica, listen to me. You will be tempted to sleep with someone on the road. Keep your eyes open."

At first, I thought that she was worrying too much. I was a professional, touring with other professionals. We were there to work. Of course I wasn't going to start sleeping around. But I learned soon enough that a lot of people, both men and women, have a hard time creating boundaries between work and play. I learned how important it was to keep the sexy in check.

Remember how I told you in the first chapter about those fine R&B singers who invited me to their room? If it wasn't for the advice of the woman from church, I might not have been prepared to handle it. As it was, though, I knew to cut off the offer before it went anywhere. I wasn't a gospel singer yet, but I knew I would be someday. And even while I was standing in that elevator, I could see the moment, years in the future, when that man would look at me and say, "I remember you . . ." And I didn't want his memory to be of me in his bed.

I knew that anyone who wanted me as a wife wouldn't want me on display for the world to see, so there were things I wouldn't wear and things I wouldn't do. Even today, I don't go to men's hotel rooms when I'm on the road; we can always meet in the lobby. If one of my male friends or colleagues starts texting my phone late at night, I'll push him back a little. "What are you doing up this late? ☺ I'll hit you tomorrow." I don't spend too much time with a guy without knowing his wife or girlfriend. I don't take long drives alone with men who aren't my husband or a family member.

Am I being overly cautious? Maybe. As my mom likes to say, I'd rather be saved from some things than out of some things. I'd rather be saved from heartaches than out of heartaches. I would rather avoid something than repent for it later.

I'm not saying that you shouldn't be friends with men or

work with men, or that all men are just trying to sleep with you. But when there's someone you spend a lot of time with, things can slowly get to a point of no return. By the time you notice, you've already crossed lines you never meant to get near. What started as a nice, pleasant conversation about something innocent grew when you noticed he had a nice smile. Then he started stopping by your desk every day to empathize about how hard one of the customers is to please. Then there was the night you both had to stay late to work, or the company event that you both had to travel for, and the conversations got personal. You started thinking about him when you weren't at work. You started anticipating your time with him. You texted him about something innocent, and he responded, and now you're talking all the time. That friendly work colleague is now filling a little bit of your desire to be desired that your husband used to hold. You may have not ever touched him, but you're already in the danger zone.

My aunt Theresa told me that the enemy will start in January to destroy you by December. So pay attention and establish yourself as a woman to be respected from the start of the friendship.

None of this is easy. Honoring your body takes time, patience, and especially discipline. But if you see yourself as worthy of being treated well, others will treat you well. You are a temple and a gift, and you deserve to be treated that way—not just by others but by yourself. You're the caretaker of a temple of God, and nothing is too good for you.

Chapter 9

Be Open to Change

If you had met sixteen-year-old Erica Atkins, it would be hard for you to imagine that she would become the Erica Campbell I am today. The church that I grew up in was amazing, as I've said—loving and grounded in God's Word and in the power of prayer. But we were also very culturally conservative. We didn't listen to non-Christian music, and women never wore pants to church. In fact, my mom still won't wear pants to church to this day, and she's not at all fond of red nail polish or red lipstick.

Then I met Warryn, who was working with a lot of R&B acts. He played keys for the singer Brandy, and when one of her singers couldn't make some of her shows, she hired me to sing backup for her. It was a great opportunity professionally, but my church family wasn't very happy about it. I was going to sing secular music! I was going to travel with non-Christians!

My dad was convinced Warryn was trying to change me from a gospel singer to an R&B singer, and my church girlfriends came to my little studio apartment and prayed for God's protection over my life. And no matter how much I protested that this was a job, and that God would be with me wherever I went, and that Brandy was just sixteen years old at the time and singing really clean music, nothing reassured them. It's still funny and sweet to think of how nervous everyone was for me.

Finally, my pastor, who is also my uncle, sat down with me. I thought for sure he was going to tell me not to go. This was the same man, after all, who a few years before had asked me why was I in a hurry to move to marry that handsome church boy, because that would mean leaving my church and choir. But he surprised me.

"I've prayed, and I think you're supposed to do this," my pastor said. "You're supposed to learn something. Go on the tour, and when you get back, come and get back in the choir." Now, in our church and our family, it was almost never okay to skip services. Being sent out into the world to experience something new was a radical decision for all of us. With his blessing, though, I went on the tour, and when it was over, I came right back to singing at church.

It was clear not everyone there saw my decision the way our pastor did, and I definitely got some side eye and concerned comments from the church ladies, especially when that tour with Brandy ended and led to tours with other artists. A few years later, Tina started traveling with R&B artists as well.

It was an eye-opening time for both of us. Singing on concert stages was a lot different than singing in church. I learned a lot, not just about how the music industry worked, but also how to operate in the mainstream world as a believer. Up to that point, Warryn will tell you that I could be pretty judgmental, and he's probably right, though I'd like to point out that I always spoke in love. If I met people who weren't Christians, I was the kind of person who would sweetly say, "Oh, you're not saved? You don't know Jesus?" And then with a concerned smile, I'd tell them that they were going to hell. Everything for me was black and white.

All of my naive but well-intentioned words, not surprisingly, didn't get far with the people who didn't even believe in hell.

But those R&B tours pushed me out of my comfort zones and started to show me how God reveals Himself in different ways and different places. For starters, I learned that the love of God draws more people than threats of condemnation. I started to understand that different churches and different individuals all worship and serve the same God in their own ways. I saw how God was with the women who avoid nail polish and makeup and with the women who got all glammed up. He was with the Christians who praise the Lord out loud with every breath, and also with the Christians who sit quiet. He speaks through all of the different translations of the Bible to those who are looking to find Him.

Despite all the worries of the people at church, I never turned away from God. I never stopped being God's girl and never stopped shining for Him. But I did discover a bigger, bolder, more wonderful perspective of who God is and how I can live with and for Him. I was changing as God prepared me for Mary Mary.

❧

I don't know what's happening in your life as you read this, but I do know this: you will be faced with changes. Where you are right now, today, is not where God will keep you forever. Who you are today isn't who you will be next month or next year. Where you thought you were going isn't always where you find yourself.

God created you to grow and mature, and He put you in a world that's full of surprises. The job that you thought you'd spend your life doing might disappear. Your child will grow up and challenge you. Your husband might get a promotion that comes with a move to a new city. A chance conversation could open your eyes to a new need in your community or in the world. You could discover a new passion, or a trial could alter the way you see the world. Every day, something will happen that has the ability to disrupt your life, and every disruption is a chance to grow as a person and as a child of God.

You were created to shift and evolve from stage to stage, and grace to grace, and challenge to challenge. With each lesson, He moves you closer to the destiny He has for you.

The question isn't what will happen; it's how you will react. Part of your soul work is learning how to navigate those shifts without losing your footing. Part of living in beauty is gracefully moving through the world even when you're entering new territory.

Those early years in music were sometimes dizzying for me, with doors opening as fast as I could move toward them, all leading to the launch and success of Mary Mary. Then, for a season, my changes were personal. Marriage. Babies. Money. As Mary Mary continued to grow and to draw new listeners and more awards, my career seemed stable. My energy was on the duo.

All of that changed a few years ago, when God showed me that it was time to step away from Mary Mary for a while. It wasn't something I went looking for, but after almost fifteen years of performing together, Tina and I found ourselves in places where our needs didn't line up the way they used to. She felt called to spend more time at home with her family. She needed a break, but I couldn't just sit back and wait until she was ready to sing again. I love what I do. I had my own dreams and calling, and I knew that God wasn't releasing me from them. Tina needed to step back, but I needed to keep moving. We had some hard conversations, and eventually agreed that it was time to take a break.

Once I freed myself and invited God to bring new opportunities to my life, the doors started to fly open again. Everywhere I looked, change happened. The solo album. The radio show. The TV show with my family. This book. I've been stretched and expanded and blessed beyond measure. At the same time, I've gone through trials. Every step has been a challenge, and there were some setbacks along the way. But in the end, God brought me to a place that's so much more fulfilling than I could have imagined.

Some of you who are reading this are a bit younger, still building your lives, and that sense of future blessings is hard to see. Maybe you aren't married but you want to be, or you're still trying to find your career path or calling. Money's tight. Your life isn't what you thought it would be. At this point, you have no idea how to move forward, but you're tired of waiting. You have a lot of questions and not many answers.

It's hard to see this when you're in the middle of it, but trust me when I say it won't always be like this.

When Tina and I first moved out, we were sharing a one-bedroom apartment that cost $500 a month, and we couldn't even afford that. I was doing hair and working to make ends meet, but my music ambitions just weren't happening fast enough. There were days when I cried, thinking I was a loser, but I knew if I moved back home it would just solidify my loserness, and I still believed He was preparing me for great things.

Your situation might be different, but your feelings are probably the same. Insecurity and the desire to become something more, and the deep need for love, acceptance, and friendship are all part of coming of age. I'm here to reassure you that generations of women have been through it before you, and we can all promise you that it won't last forever.

There was a song I listened to a lot during those challenging days called "Count It All Joy," by The Winans. Maybe I didn't have many dollars to count, I reasoned, but God had given me plenty of joy. And after all, as Tina once said, "We're not poor. We just don't have some things." Classic Tina.

We'd spent our whole lives without material stuff or financial security, and yet God continued to care for us. He made us strong and taught us the value of work. We didn't have much, but we had food every day and a roof over our heads. We laughed and sang and played. We had two parents who loved us. We had family, faith, and Jesus.

What about you? What has God given you? I guarantee that if you're seeking Him, He's given you something to work with. Look back to the verse in Proverbs that says, "Trust in the Lord with all your heart, and lean not on your own understanding; in all your ways acknowledge Him, and He shall direct your paths." I love the word *shall* there, because it's such a bold promise. There's no question mark. It's not He *might* direct your path, or He *can* direct your path, or He *could* direct your path. No, if you commit to God and His plans, He commits to you. He *shall* provide everything you need.

So if your life isn't what you want it to be yet, refuse to identify with your current situation. If your heart is lonely or your wallet is empty or you still can't find a job that means something, don't get stuck there. Don't make rash decisions or tattoo your feelings on your life. Don't beat yourself up or abuse yourself. Tell yourself, "This is where I am, but not who I am." God has already made the provision for a change in your circumstances, and if you bring the faith and the push, He'll bring the results.

You won't be here forever. Like my mom told me after that broken engagement, you can live anything down. Just keep going. Wake up another day and bring your best self. Do the work. Get disciplined. Speak life. Make a plan.

He *shall* direct you. You're going to be able to pay your bills. You're going to be loved. You're going to be successful somewhere. You're going to become wiser with age. I don't know when or how, but I know it's going to happen for you if you remain open to Him. The Bible assures us that He has made everything you'll ever need available to you. Life is going to continue to unfold the layers of your story in ways you can't imagine yet.

God's plan is so much more creative than anything you could dream for yourself.

Tina and I toured with R&B groups right up until Mary Mary launched and "Shackles" took off. After that, we thought, okay, now it's time for us to minister to the church. We were singing gospel music, and so we assumed that we were going to mainly encourage believers.

But God had some different plans. From the start, we told our record company that we wanted to sing for the world. Seriously. When they asked me who I thought Mary Mary's audience was, I said "everyone in the world."

So when "Shackles" became such a big song worldwide, Tina and I were invited to perform at big events and festivals alongside a variety of artists, including rappers like Lil' Kim and

Snoop Dogg, or rock bands like U2 and Bon Jovi. Those weren't the kind of performances I thought we were going to have, but we were obedient to go wherever God led us and to trust that He would show up. And He did. At some events, Tina and I would wait backstage while Sisqó sang "Thong Song," and then we'd be next on stage, singing "Thank You, Lord." And every time, at every show, there were people in the audience who would raise their hands or dance and sing and praise the Lord with us. At the end of the night, there was usually someone who would come up and thank us. They'd tell us how long it had been since they'd prayed or talked to God, and how much they missed gospel music and wanted to go back to church.

When I was a teenager, I used to go with my dad and sing when he preached at street and prison ministries. I have a heart for reaching people who don't speak Christianese and who don't go to church every Sunday, but still, I kept wondering when Mary Mary was going to start singing in the churches and more traditional spaces. We were gospel artists, after all. Shouldn't we be singing with the believers?

It was our friend and fellow musician Donnie McClurkin who finally said the thing that set me straight. "I'm called to the kingdom," he told me, "but maybe Mary Mary is called to the world. There are people who will hear you who would never hear me, and you can be the ones to make that first introduction to Jesus."

Looking back, that conversation was another moment of change for me, because it brought me freedom to live and work in the spaces God brought to me, rather than trying to force myself onto paths that I thought would please God and church people. God put the doors in front of me, and it was my job to open them and walk through.

Are you creating the space in your life for God to bring the changes He has for you? Or are you holding onto all of the things in your past that once defined you?

In my group of friends, we always seemed to fall into certain roles. We had the bossy friend, the goofy friend, the one who is always late, and the forgetful friend. That was me, the forgetful friend. I'd let all kinds of plans slip by and just never show up. As the years went by, our group of friends started to make jokes about our different roles. And they'd always tell me, "Well, we know you're going to forget about this."

Just about the time that Mary Mary was starting to take off, one of our friends asked me to do her a favor and deliver something to a music executive. And, well, I was busy, and that package stayed in my trunk for months. Eventually, my friend took it personally. "I know you're forgetful, but if you didn't want to do it for me, all you had to do is say so."

Up to that point, as I've told you, I didn't speak up very often. I was the one who went along to get along. But I was getting older, and I was doing my own soul work, and something inside me was ready for a change.

I let her know my opinion. I told her I was working hard, and though I had the best intentions I was very busy, and that she was requiring a lot of me. And while I was at it, I asked them all to stop declaring this forgetfulness over my life. "You know I don't want to forget. I apologize for the times I haven't been there. I don't want to be your forgetful friend. I don't want that to be my label, so please, I need you to stop saying that about me when I'm trying not to be that person anymore."

It was a lot for me to say all at once, and the word got around. My girlfriends were calling me to ask, "Did you really say that?" Everybody was blown away. But I was growing up, and I told my friends I wanted them to grow up with me. For years, I'd been the floater, and I never felt the need to stand up for myself. But at this point in my life, sometimes there were going to be things I wanted and things I didn't want, and I should be free to speak my truth.

My friends all heard me, because they're amazing women, and they said okay, let's get to know this new Erica. Let's give her a chance to change and be someone new. And it was a little awkward at first, and there were some growing pains, but we're all stronger now because they gave me space and let me mature and change. It was an important moment for all of us.

There is a season for everything, it says in the book of Ecclesiastes, and what I take from that is that things will not always stay the same. If you spend all of your time trying to hold onto the past or obsessing about what happened "back then," there's no room for God to bring you a new future.

Oh, but Erica, this thing that happened to me ten years ago changed everything, you say. And I'm sure it did. Something or someone radically changed your direction. But that was ten years ago. You've celebrated ten Thanksgivings, ten birthdays, and ten Christmases since then, and today is a new day. What is God calling you to look at now, and into the future? Don't get stuck on the past. You are a whole new person.

And it's not just you who is new. The people around you are new, too.

Parents learn this the hard way, as our children grow and launch off in new directions. Being the mother of a teenager means that I'm in a constant state of change, learning to let go and help my child grow into herself on a daily basis. Krista is not the same today as she was a month ago, and I know from watching my friends with older kids that this process of letting go and letting grow will keep stretching me for a while. I can't hold her back. I can't try to keep her young and dependent. God has all sorts of plans for her, and my job is to help her become the woman who can accomplish them.

If there are people around you who are trying to change, let them. If your brother is working hard to rebuild his life after a mistake, don't keep reminding him of who he used to be. If your friend is establishing herself as a responsible professional, don't keep reminding her of the embarrassing things she did as a teenager.

It's time for something new, for all of us.

A lot of the time, getting to change means fighting past the darkness. You've got to push through pain and adversity to achieve your new start. Maybe it was a breakup or a death, or a loss of finances or a job or a house. Maybe it was the devastation of a betrayal or the loss of a friendship.

Whatever it is, you have to lose something in order to create the space for something new. I know it's kind of a cliché to say, but really, everything that doesn't kill you makes you stronger. And God needs strong people in His army.

Tina and I wrote a song for Mary Mary that we called "Dirt," and the first verse and chorus say:

Funny thing about a garden
Beauty lives within its gates
Bugs and thorns and weeds, they grow there
But they all help to create
Vivid color variations
Sweet aromas and sensations
Realize under it all, there's something not so beautiful
But we all need a little bit of dirt to grow
We need a little rain to wash our souls

We couldn't have known when we wrote that song more than ten years ago how much the words would resonate with so many people today. Or how much, once again, God would call on us to live out the words we wrote for the stage. Today, I think that we both understand how much mud a flower has to push through before it bursts into the sunlight and blooms. There have been things that could break us down or take us down, but the words of that song still shone bright. The rain washed our souls, and God helped us bloom.

Don't be afraid of the tragedy in your life, if you have one. It might be the thing that God will use to take you to greatness. "All things are possible to him who believes," Jesus says in Mark 9:23. And in Joshua 1:9, God says, "Be strong and of good courage; do not be afraid, nor be dismayed, for the Lord your God is with you wherever you go."

I'll always remember a story I heard about a guy named Kevin D. Morton, who in 2007 was a twenty-two-year-old college student in Detroit when, at the end of his shift managing a restaurant, a robber shot him in the stomach. His wounds were bad, and the doctors said he had just a 10 percent chance of surviving. But there was a surgeon on call that night who saw his potential and went the extra mile, and Kevin survived. He was in the intensive care unit for six weeks, and couldn't have solid food for a whole year. But he didn't give up. He went back to college and graduated, and then went to medical school. Ten years after he entered the emergency room as a patient, he came back to the same hospital to work as a doctor and return the favor.

Ten years is a long time. The process of change might seem slow. Some steps might even seem impossible. You'll be tempted at times to say that what you're facing is too hard, too steep, asks too much of you. But when you're holding onto God's hand and following His directions, you'll make it. And as you look back at that step and think "huh, that trial didn't take me out," your perspective changes a little. Your sense of what you can accomplish and what you can do expands.

My dad loved to quote Proverbs 24:10, "If you faint in the day of adversity, your strength is small." But God created you to be strong. You will face your days of adversity, but the new life of deeper joy and contentment that you're longing for is on the other side.

Are there questions that drive you crazy? You know, like how every time you go to a wedding, if you're single all of the older women ask, "Are you dating someone? Will your wedding be next?" Or then, as soon as you get married, everyone starts to ask, "When are you going to have kids?"

How's that job hunt going? Are you going to buy a house? When are you going to retire? When are your kids going to make you a grandma?

Whatever season of life you're in, someone's always ready to push you toward something else, whether you want to go there or not, or else they're trying to stop you from going somewhere you want to go. Why would you start a business when you could get a nice, stable, normal job? What do you mean you're going on a missions trip?

Not everyone was on board with Mary Mary's position as a gospel group who sang in unorthodox arenas. We got our share of pushback from the church people who thought we were selling out somehow, and the wider world that thought we were too Jesus-y. I don't think there is a song that I've put out, either as a solo artist or as Mary Mary, that someone didn't challenge. Every single has gotten someone saying, "Well, that's not really what we put on the radio; that's not our style."

But I push and I push, and I pray and I pray, and my music found its audience. I'm here today because no one can do what I do quite the same as the way I do it. And no one can do what you do, either.

I love Psalm 139:14, which says, "I will praise You, for I am fearfully and wonderfully made; Marvelous are Your works, and that my soul knows very well."

God fearfully and wonderfully made you as a unique person, with your own calling and talent. He has set out for you a purpose and a path that is different from every other person in the universe. Your future is full of special and wonderful surprises. And so it's possible that He's going to call you to forge new territory. He might ask you to do something that no one else has done before.

Are you ready for that? Because here's the thing about following God's calling: it's not about what other people think. If God calls you to leave what is comfortable and go into a new place, go. If no one around you supports the vision He gave you, persevere. Or on the other side, if God tells you to wait, to rest, to be patient even if everyone around you is getting carried away by a new thing, listen.

When I have to make a decision that will disappoint people, I think a lot about the apostle Paul, who always acted so that he was in line with his own conscience, subject to God and the Holy Spirit, even if he wasn't in line with the other church leaders of his day. He was in a season of persecution, and he said it over and over again. "I have lived in all good conscience before God until this day," he told the council of church leaders when they interrogated him about his conversion. "I tell the truth in Christ, I am not lying, my conscience also bearing me witness in the Holy Spirit," he told the Romans. No matter what anyone else thought about him, Paul stood well before the Lord, because his conscience was right with the Holy Spirit.

You're never going to please all of the people all of the time. You might not even please the people who are closest to you. But if your eyes are on God and you're following the directions in which He leads you, you'll please Him, and that's what matters most.

If God has called you to something and the people around you say "but no one else has ever done that," then take it as a good sign. You're on track to be new and innovative. As long as it doesn't go against the will or the Word of God, live your life and do your thing.

Is there something tugging at your heart, calling out for you to go in a new direction? Is the Holy Spirit whispering to your soul that He has something bigger and better for you?

If there is a change that your heart desires and the Holy Spirit confirms that it's in line with the will of God, own it. Name it. If you want to see change in your life, now is the time to acknowledge that. If you have been avoiding change that you know needs to happen, now is the time to stop fighting that and tell God, directly and honestly, that you're ready.

And then have the faith that He will provide.

God alone is able to bring new life and new direction to any situation. He's able to redeem what seems unredeemable, and mend what seems forever broken. He promises over and over that He will provide what you need and guide you toward fulfilling the dreams He has for you. When the Lord is your shepherd, the psalmist says, you shall not want. "He makes me to lie down in green pastures; He leads me beside the still waters. He restores my soul."

But He won't act alone. Remember, God doesn't do anything for you without you. You have to do your part, which means listening to the leading of the Holy Spirit first, then spending time in the Word and in prayer to make sure that you're in line with what God desires, and then having the faith to move forward in full confidence.

When you walk into a meeting, does your mind say, *I hope they'll receive what I want to say*? *I hope I'm not going to bother anyone or impose on them*? Or do you go in there with boldness? If you approach a conversation or a new opportunity with a spirit of timidity, your hesitation will spread. But if you go in knowing who you are and with the strength of the Holy Spirit and confidence in the promises of God, then you will be treated as someone with purpose and value.

Hebrews 11:1 reminds us that "faith is the substance of things hoped for, the evidence of things not seen." Faith is the certainty that something is real, even when you can't see it. It's the confidence that God will keep His promises and work "all things . . . together for good to those who love God, to those who are the called according to His purpose," as it says in Romans 8.

You use your faith every day. Getting out of bed is an act of faith that the floor under your feet will hold you up when you stand. But what about when it comes to the big things? Have faith that God will hold you up when you step out into a new career, or move to a new city, or start a new program. If you accept a challenge, believe that He will be there with you. The changes that are coming in your life will stretch your comfort zones, test your courage, and a lot of times bring you through times of adversity. Other people may doubt your vision. Your faith is what will keep you focused on what God has for you.

"Thanks be to God," says Paul in 1 Corinthians 15:57, "who gives us the victory through our Lord Jesus Christ." At the end of every service at California Worship Center, we all stand and join hands across the aisles. And together, we declare, "Lord, I thank you for the week ahead. It is a week of victory." We say it three times, getting louder each time, with our hands raised.

Change is coming to your life, whether you want it or not. Take victory with you. Victory is powerful and strong; victory is bold and big. The changes in your life can lead you to victory. When you invite it into your life, things will happen.

Chapter 10

Pass It On

My oldest daughter, Krista, is fourteen. It's a tough age—too big to be little and too little to be big. It's that season of life when you want to be independent and adult, but you don't really know enough about life yet. You don't even really know yourself yet.

As a parent, one of my priorities has always been to make time to talk to each one of my kids about their lives. I want them to know that they can tell me anything, that I'm a safe place. And so Krista and I have talked a lot about how she feels about growing up: about boys and friends and faith and mean girls and herself. My daughter is working through the same questions about beauty and identity that we've all asked. *Am I good enough? Am I pretty enough? Am I talented? Does anyone value me?*

Of course, I always tell her yes, she's beautiful and has an incredible voice, and I try to explain that the boys will come. I tell her she's going to grow into her sexiness someday, but hopefully not too soon. I tell her about how I used to talk to my mom about some of these same things, and how my mom always loved me, just as I will always love Krista. I promise her that we're going to walk through it all together.

I don't know if she really believes me yet, because when you're fourteen it's hard to believe that your mom knows anything, but I know she's listening.

One night, I was in the kitchen, cleaning up and putting dishes away and doing things to get ready for the next day. Krista was at the table, looking at something on her phone, when all of a sudden she said, "You're a good mommy."

"I am?" I asked her, because I didn't know how else to respond. "What made you say that?"

"Because you care about me and let me talk," she said. "You don't let me get away with stuff, but you don't minimize what I think. You never make me feel like what I'm saying isn't important."

That hit my heart like a ton of bricks. As a woman whose job involves travel, I live with a lot of mommy guilt. Am I ruining my kids because I'm not around enough? Am I spending enough time with them? Am I paying enough attention when I am home with them? Am I helping them grow toward Jesus? I reprimand myself a lot. Nobody can beat up on Erica Campbell better than I can.

But then Krista says something like that, or Warryn III calls and leaves a message on my phone that just says, "I love you, Mommy. I hope you're doing good. Was your show good today? Call me." And my heart gets all warm, and I start to think that maybe Warryn and I are doing okay as parents after all.

God uses my kids to bring me new understanding of what it means to live as someone who knows she's more than pretty. My soul work doesn't stop when I've got my own life in order. I've also got to communicate what I've learned to the people around me, starting with my family. I can't come here and write to you about how much God values you if my own daughter doesn't know it. I can't go to church and help the women there believe in themselves if my own kids are struggling with self-acceptance. I've got to live this More Than Pretty message in the Campbell house first, or else I'm a fraud.

"Diligently keep yourself, lest you forget the things your eyes have seen, and lest they depart from your heart," Moses told the Israelites in Deuteronomy 4:9. Then he said, "Teach them to your children and your grandchildren."

If I interviewed your kids, would they say that their mommy is strong? That she takes care of herself and surrounds herself with people who love and guide her? If I talked to your sisters or closest girlfriends, would they tell me that you're sure of your purpose and full of the Word of God?

Once you've uncovered your own purpose and calling, God calls you to live that truth out loud. Pass your blessings on to your kids, and share your wisdom with the people around you— your brothers and sisters and friends and nieces and nephews. They've got hearts that are struggling to be seen, too.

I'm going to talk a lot to moms in this chapter, because helping our daughters see themselves as more than pretty is such a big issue, and we all have questions about how to be good parents. But if you're not a mother, don't quit on me just yet. You have your own opportunities to build up other women and help them see their beauty, prettiness, sexiness, and identity. You can open doors for all kinds of people God brings into your path.

This is a place where we all need to stand together as sisters.

"I always feel like somebody's watching me." Remember that song from the '80s? It was kind of funny back then, but there's truth in those words. You are on display. Your words and actions are being watched—by your kids, your family, your neighbors, your coworkers, and even the random person who sees you losing your cool in the grocery store.

I've talked a lot already about my aunt Theresa, the first lady of my church and one of the classiest women I know. Aunt Theresa isn't famous and she isn't rich, but she's always been my role model, a powerful woman I watched and learned from. I still do. She's in her seventies now, still cute and sassy and flirtatious with her husband. She's the perfect example of the verse in Ephesians that says, "See then that you walk circumspectly, not as fools but as wise."

Even in the painful times, I saw how Aunt Theresa never broke. "It doesn't feel good, but I'm a lady," she'd tell me. And so when my life hit its own bumps and bruises, I would tell myself, "It doesn't feel good, but I can get through it because I'm a tough lady like Aunt Theresa."

Wherever you are, someone's watching you like I watched

Aunt Theresa. When you're driving and think that the kids in the backseat aren't paying attention, they are. When you're walking through a store or sitting in the back row at church and you think everyone is too wrapped up in themselves to notice you, someone will. Whether you're eighteen or eighty, there are people looking and comparing what they see in you to how they're living.

If you struggled in the past to see your value, it may be hard to imagine that anyone notices you. If the enemy tricked you into thinking that you weren't "pretty" enough to be visible, then you may have thought you were flying under the radar all these years. That no one was paying attention. But even your insecurity was noticed. If you treated yourself as someone who isn't worthy, that's how the people around you probably treated you, too.

But now you've seen how much you are loved. You are more than pretty. You are valuable, and you are talented, and you are destined to make a difference in this world. That should change not just the way you look in the mirror, but also the way you act, which will change the way that other people see you.

Your words, especially, have incredible power. Even your most casual comment or behavior can make a lasting impact on another person. I used to talk about my weight a lot at home, but I don't do it anymore because I realized that Krista was listening to me, and starting to say critical things about herself. I don't talk at home about how stressed out I feel or complain about how hard something is, because then my kids will start thinking that it's okay to complain when things are hard. Instead, I make a conscious decision to let my children see and hear me declare what God's Word says about me regardless of how I feel.

When you're committed to integrity, respect, and love, your influence will change lives.

I'll always remember the day my mom found out that I'd had sex. I was eighteen years old, and one of my girlfriends from church had told my older cousin, and that cousin—scared I would get pregnant—told my mom. One afternoon while we were driving in her 1990 blue Chevy Celebrity, my mom asked me flat out if I was having sex. "Tell me it's not true, baby."

I couldn't lie to my mama, so I confessed. I waited for her to launch into a lecture, or scream at me and fill me with shame, but she never did. Even when she was faced with her "good girl" daughter's poor choices, her loving presence never faltered. She controlled her temper and her disappointment, she forgave, and she loved on me so much in that car that I walked away determined to return that love by returning to her rules and guidelines.

That's the power that a person's words and actions can have when they're covered with love.

I know how lucky I am to have been raised by two parents who both loved Jesus and strove to serve Him. They weren't perfect, but their influence always kept me grounded in the things that mattered.

My mom's favorite verse is Joshua 24:15, and especially the part that says "as for me and my house, we will serve the Lord." That was the foundation of the Atkins household. We all went to church every Sunday, and we all read the Bible together, and we all prayed together. There was no fighting back on this, or deciding we didn't feel like it one day.

When Warryn and I got serious about dating, as I've said, my dad had concerns about Warryn's music and lifestyle. He was sure that this young man was going to lead me away from the church. That's a funny thing to think about now, when I watch Pastor Warryn on stage preaching every Sunday, but at the time my dad was serious, and he needed reassuring.

"Do you believe you did a good job raising me?" I asked him. He said yes.

"Do you believe you taught me the things I need to know?" He said yes again.

"Then there's your answer," I said. "Don't worry about whether you can trust Warryn or even whether you trust me. Trust what you taught me. Trust that you did such a good job that your daughter heard you, because I did. Even if my road is different than yours, I'm always, absolutely, one hundred percent listening to you and Mommy. You raised me to know right from wrong, and I know Warryn's not going to try to take me out of the church."

If you are a parent, never underestimate your importance. You hold someone's tender soul in your hands. It doesn't matter if your child is a baby or an adult or somewhere in between. It doesn't matter if your children are rebellious or shy or sweet or sulking. They long for your love and approval, and the way you act and interact with them will shape them forever.

Don't believe me? Look at your friends who were raised as their parents' favorite child, compared to those who weren't. (Yes, some parents have favorites, and even if they can't admit it, everyone in the family knows it. It's hard, but it's true.) The adults I know who were favorites all have this natural confidence. They go out into the world knowing they are loved and believing that they will be seen. But many of those who were not given as much of their parents' positive attention became aggressive adults. They're bigger talkers and bigger personalities, as if they're always trying to prove their value and making sure that someone really sees them.

Children need public affirmation, consistent love, and support from their parents. Even Jesus, when He lived on earth as a human, had that need. When He was baptized by John the Baptist, both Matthew and Mark report that the sky opened and a voice came from heaven: "This is my beloved Son, in whom I am well pleased."

We know that nothing in the Bible is there without reason, and I think that God's public blessing is there to show us how important a parent's affirmation is. Jesus was both fully divine and fully human, with human needs. He got hungry. He needed a nap. He wanted to get away sometimes. Hearing His father say that He was pleased in Him must have meant everything.

Can you imagine how different the people around you would

be if they all knew that their fathers were proud of them and that their mothers loved them? When children don't feel that, they're left with a deep longing, a need that has to be fulfilled some other way. You've probably known your share of people who grew up without a mom or dad, or with a parent trapped in some kind of struggle that robbed them of the ability to be present for their kids. Those people are always searching for something.

If that's your story growing up, I hope that you've learned how to fill that need with God's love, which can cover every need you have. I hope that no matter how old you are, you have surrogate parents in your community, elders like my aunt Theresa who can guide you lovingly and fill you with affirmation. I hope you find mentors who are tough on you and challenge you to be your best. Being a parentless child is something that you can overcome.

But God's plan is clear, and the best source of spiritual guidance and natural resiliency comes from the people who share your home and your blood. So if you are blessed with children, take that responsibility seriously. Build a bond, and make it a priority to help them find their own beauty and strength.

Here's a place to start: Pray together as a family, every day and as often as you can. Pray out loud, so your kids can hear you, and encourage them to pray out loud with you as soon as they're old enough to talk. You don't have to be formal or fancy. It doesn't have to be something you've got all planned out or scheduled. If something sad happens, stop and ask God for comfort. If you're trying to figure something out, tell your kids, "Let's pray about it." If you're happy about something, "Well, let's thank God for it."

When your children learn to pray, they learn how to deal with life's surprises and setbacks. When they pray, they'll be reminded that they are never alone, and are always loved. And they might just surprise you.

A couple of years ago, I made the mistake of taking all three kids to the mall. We'd already had a full day of practices and rehearsals, so everyone was tired and my patience was thin. But Warryn III needed new shoes for church and Zaya needed socks, and I told myself it would be fine.

Well, we got into the store, and my kids started being kids. Krista picked out some stuff, and Zaya got mad because she couldn't have as much as Krista, and so there was one kid antagonizing and one kid crying, and then Warryn III wandered off instead of sitting down to try on shoes. And I snapped into mean mama mode. You know the type. "Get yourself over here and sit down. Don't touch nothing else. Don't harass your sister. Y'all are getting on my nerves."

I may have raised my voice just a little bit at Zaya, which I don't usually do, and that made her cry harder. "Mommy, why are you talking so loud?"

By the time we got to the car, I was beyond frustrated. The kids were scared. The whole scene was falling apart until Krista, all of twelve years old at the time, reached over and grabbed my hand. "Lord, in the name of Jesus, touch my mommy and let her be calm. Give her peace and don't let her be frustrated or upset. Lord, let her enjoy her time with us and let us enjoy our time with her. In Jesus' name, amen."

My sweet Krista's prayer shifted the mood of everyone in the car, and I drove out of the parking lot just shaking my head and smiling so big. I've always known the verse in Proverbs 22 that says, "Train up a child in the way he should go, and when he is old, he will not depart from it." I just didn't realize that "old" would start at twelve!

When you create a culture of faith in your house, you let your children see how God's plans and God's desires infuse every corner of life. When you pray with them and in front of them, and when they see you reading your Bible and studying God's Word, these things naturally become part of how they live their own lives.

The same goes for church and fellowship with other believers.

Not long ago, someone asked Warryn if it was ever okay to bribe her reluctant or rebellious children to get them to go to church. He responded, "Do you bribe them to eat well? Do you bribe them to go to school? Do you have to trick your children into doing the other things that help them become their best selves? Why should you feel like you have to make excuses or ask for favors for something that will potentially change your child's life forever?"

When we're talking about how to share God's love and care with your kids, I think Scripture is pretty clear about the importance of the fellowship of believers. You do them a great disservice when you don't require that your whole family get involved with a church, and I don't say that just because I'm a first lady.

When Warryn and I started a family, long before he felt called to start a church, we agreed that church wouldn't be optional for the Campbells. This was where our family would grow, and where we would worship, and where we would serve. And with our kids in tow, he and I made it a point to get and stay connected. Our bishop became our spiritual leader, and the people in the congregation became our friends. When Sunday rolls around, our kids never question that this is where we're going to be.

If your children are resisting the body of believers, start by going back and asking that *why* question. Are they getting messages from their friends? Is there something about this specific church that doesn't fit? Or is there a negative message that they're picking up from you? A lot of adults end up carrying bitterness or hard feelings toward a church or church member from their past. Maybe you had a boring pastor, or your parents treated church like a punishment and not a gift. If so, and you're treating church like an obligation, then don't be surprised that that's what your kids think, too.

If you act like church is something you'd rather avoid, then your kids will get that message. If you drop them off for Sunday school but don't stay yourself, they'll get the idea that this isn't a desirable place to be. But if you find a church and a community that's full of passion and offers them love, then you won't have to trick them into getting involved. If you're excited about the chance to learn more about a sovereign and loving and holy God who is in control of the universe, and wants to be close to you, then that's what you'll pass along to your family.

When I was a child, I was surrounded by a whole village of church people who told me, "You're going to be great one day. You're not like everybody else, Erica. You aren't like the other kids. There's something special about you. Stick with it, baby."

Those words pushed me to keep at it, even when I wanted to quit the choir and go play outside with my friends. As I got older, I wanted to turn off the spotlight sometimes, but I didn't. I rested instead on the knowledge that I was living the fulfillment of what my amazing church family had always seen in me. When they come to my concerts today, I get all choked up to see them beaming with pride. Every time I win something or achieve something, it's due in part to the love that they showered on me back then.

When you fill kids with love like those elders gave to me, you build up their inner strength and resolve. When you speak words of life over them, affirming their future and pointing them toward their destiny, you create a core identity that they can call on when they face trials or temptations.

Warryn and I started speaking into our children's lives when they were babies. We told each of them that they were going to be awesome. We'd cradle them and whisper, "You're going to be strong, you're going to be smart, you're going to have a great relationship with God." We overloaded them with affirmation, because we wanted them to always know that whatever happened out in the world, they would be safe and loved and valued. We speak life still today so that they understand how worthy and beautiful they are. Between these walls, we believe that they can do anything and conquer anything. Nothing is too hard, because God is on their side.

Yes, they will still deal with devastation, and I prepare them for that. My children will face bullies, and people will say things that are cruel and untrue. Their hearts will probably be broken a time or two. I can't protect them from everything, but I can make sure that they have the strength and the resources to face it. After all, even bullies serve a purpose in God's greater plan.

I tell my kids that sometimes we need a bully to draw out the greatness in us. We wouldn't know who David was without Goliath. And so if someone challenges them or tries to belittle them, I want my kids to be so full of love that the words don't penetrate. I want them to have skin thick enough to protect them from lies, and a strong voice to defend themselves. If someone tells them that they're not worthy, I want them to be bold and follow their calling anyway. I want them to always understand that human beings don't see what God sees, and that outside voices that try to make them doubt their true worth can be defeated.

Speaking life isn't just an exercise for kids, though. Your whole community, and your whole world, needs encouragement. Every person, regardless of their age, desires love and assurance that they are a unique, loved, and beautiful child of God. We all want someone to recognize our talents and pray for our challenges. When we are built up, the criticism of the outside world will mean nothing.

In our More Than Pretty women's ministry at California Worship Center, we do what I call "same grace prayers," an idea I borrowed from my friend and author Priscilla Shirer. When we're all gathered together, I'll ask, "Who has a strong marriage?" Some women will raise their hands. And then I'll say, "Whose marriage is struggling?" Other women will raise their hands. The women who are blessed in that area take the hands of the women who are struggling, and they pray that God will grant those women the same blessing and grace that He's given them.

Then we look for women who have experienced the gift of physical healing and those who are struggling with their health, and then those with broken family relationships and those with strong connections to their kids and their parents. We keep going until most women have a chance both to be prayed for and to pray for others.

The whole experience is powerful, because a lot of times, the exercise challenges women to open themselves to one another, both as a giver and as a receiver, in ways that they don't normally do. It shows them how to pass on their blessings.

Connecting with other people and building their confidence in themselves starts with showing them that they deserve to be heard. Encouraging others—whether it's your child or your coworker—to own their story, to express themselves, to trust you, and to talk about whatever is on their minds empowers them to believe in their own voice. It doesn't always have to be something deep and spiritual. Maybe somebody just needs to talk about her rough day or her challenges with being single. All they need is for you to show up.

You don't even need to have answers. It's okay to say, "I don't know, but I'll pray about it with you." It's okay to let your kids and your friends see that you don't have it all together. Your presence alone is enough to give them a voice.

Every day, you have a choice: you can fill your world with affirmations and hope, or you can slide into society's pattern of grumbling and complaining over every little thing.

Proverbs 17:22 says, "A merry heart does good, like medicine, but a broken spirit dries the bones."

Sure, we live in a culture of negativity, where throwing shade is more popular than speaking kindly. The examples of family relationships we see on TV and in the media are almost always sharp-tongued and disrespectful. Fathers are minimized and disregarded, mothers are stressed, and kids seem to be running the show. Social media encourages otherwise respectful people to judge and rip apart total strangers. But that negative spirit doesn't make the world better for anyone. The more we stay angry all the time and build walls between ourselves, the more the enemy wins and the more our children suffer.

Negativity is contagious. What you exude is what you draw

in, so if you're exuding an angry or bitter spirit, or you're always complaining and always frustrated, you're giving the people around you permission to complain and be negative toward you. If you get all worked up in traffic, or belittle your husband, or call that politician or celebrity a bunch of names, the people around you, especially your kids, will start showing signs of a negative spirit, as well. If you regularly talk trash and gossip about people, then your kids will learn to look for the worst in others. If they see you fussing all the time, they're going to fuss.

Is that really what you want? Are you happy living in a world of insults instead of intimacy? And are you okay with your kids growing up there? If your kids grumble and complain and talk back to you, then that's how they'll be at school. If they're pessimists or rebellious at home, they're going to be rebellious at work someday, and they're going to bring their negativity into their other relationships. A broken spirit will follow them and limit them for years to come.

It doesn't have to be that way. You always have a choice in what you bring to every situation. The Holy Spirit is always strong enough to help you find the positive. There are kind people on this earth who need your smile, and no matter how stressed you feel, it doesn't cost anything to be nice. It doesn't diminish you to say thank you. When you're in the grocery store or walking down the street, offer a stranger a kind look or word, and watch how God will bring that action back to you tenfold. What you put out into the world will come back to you. Offering joy can help you rediscover your joy.

Now, maybe you want to smile but life has taken all of the joy from you, or you want your family to be kind but can't quite get there yourself, because so many people have taken advantage of you in the past. You think I'm having another one of those "Alice in Wonderland" moments here, because I believe in hope.

I get that things have been hard, and people have hurt you. But go back to the chapter about letting go. If you keep carrying these wounds forward, nurturing them and treating pain as your pet, it's not just going to hurt you. It's going to be what you pass on to everyone around you, especially your kids. Being mean and suspicious all the time is not an easier way to live. It's not better for you, and it's sure not better for your family.

Don't crush your child's spirit before it has the chance to grow. Don't teach your sisters that the world is a dark or terrible place, because most of it isn't. Let them be hopeful. Let them see miracles. Your experiences are not theirs. Don't let your past dry up their bones.

Does it seem like I'm asking a lot from you in this chapter, and in this book? Not only are you rediscovering your own identity, but now you're also sharing it with others? Stepping up and letting your inner self shine through your parenting and your friendships and your relationships?

It's no small thing. I warned you back in the beginning that this path to more than pretty wasn't easy. Soul work is hard work. But here's the other thing I know: you can do it. God called you to this place, and He doesn't call us without equipping us.

That's something I forgot the first time that Warryn asked me to share the stage with him at California Worship Center. He wanted me to preach, but the whole idea of teaching Scripture sent me into little-girl insecure land. In fact, I threw a full-on tantrum and stormed out the front door. I walked all over the neighborhood that afternoon, fussing at God.

"I told you I didn't want to pastor," I prayed. I was a singer. I didn't have the education or the speaking skills to get up and share the Word of God like that. I wasn't prepared; I didn't have the information. A preacher should be more talkative, more expressive, more educated. I wasn't equipped. My excuses went on and on.

Eventually, though, I ran out of words and started to listen. The Holy Spirit, who had been waiting patiently all along, told me that I wouldn't do this with my own knowledge or qualifications. I would do it through His strength. He reminded me that God hadn't just left me on my own to become a recording artist, or a parent, or a radio host, or to start a church. At every step of the way, He was there. With every change or new challenge, the Holy Spirit filled me and showed me how to do the new thing. With every change He called on me to make, He put great people around me to support me. For more than twenty years of my public ministry, the Spirit reminded me, God had done everything He said He would do. And every time I said yes, He blessed me.

By the time I got back to the house, I knew that I was being called to push myself forward in new ways once again. God was whispering words to my heart about living in beauty and spiritual confidence, about being strong in the face of trials and positive in how we approach the world. These were messages that had been swirling in my head for years, things I wanted to say to the women and girlfriends and sisters in my life.

He equipped me for my purpose, and that's how I know that He's equipped you as well. This isn't some fairy tale or pie-in-the-sky self-help book of promises. This is real. I pray that as you have read the pages of this book, you've found more than just some stories about Erica Campbell's life. I pray that you found yourself, and at some point said, "That's just where I am!" I pray that you found tools that will help you grow and blossom in your own life.

God has given us the opportunity to take a fresh look at ourselves together. He's called you to dig into His word, and your story, and the world around you. He's promised you a path to the destiny He planned for you.

You are more than pretty. You are a beautiful, strong daughter of a King.

How will you share that with the world?

Epilogue

My father battled health issues his whole life, but when he was diagnosed with cancer, none of us thought it would take his life. We prayed for healing and deliverance, and I truly believed it would happen. But God had other plans. It was May when my father was diagnosed, and in June my sister called to tell me that he'd died. It was such a shock for all of us.

When it was time to lay my dad to rest, we wanted to honor him in the biggest possible way. Our family organized a beautiful musical celebration, full of prayer and dancing and singing, and we invited dozens of people to come and share how Elder Eddie Aaron Atkins Jr. touched their lives. They came from all over, and their stories spanned his life. There wasn't a dry eye in the house, but there was also so much laughter and gratitude.

Tina and I happened to be recording a season of the *Mary Mary* TV show at the time, and so our film crew was there to follow us through the day. At the end of the celebration, one of our camera guys came up to me. "This was the most *jubilant* funeral I've ever seen. How does a person die like this? How can a funeral have this much joy?"

All I could tell him was, "If you want to die like this, you have to live like my dad did. You have to live a life that mattered and that blessed other people."

Since then, I've started to drive Warryn a little crazy by talking about my own funeral. It's not that I want to die—I'm having a great time right here on God's earth. My kids are healthy. My marriage is strong. My mom is still here. I still have music to make and stories to tell. I wake up every morning knowing that I'm blessed, grateful for another opportunity to get closer to being the person God designed me to be. I have another chance to be healthy and to help others.

But losing my dad made me face the fact that it will end eventually. By the time people are in their forties, they might have fewer years ahead of them than they do behind them. Because I believe in heaven and that I'll go there and spend eternity with Jesus, the idea of death isn't something I dread. But I do want to die right, and to do that I need to live right.

None of that is what makes Warryn crazy, though. What he doesn't like is that I'm planning my own funeral, and I'm planning it big. I'm determined that my celebration will be jam-packed, just like my dad's was, with people who have good memories of a sister and mother and woman who loved deeply and lived fully. And so I'm always telling my husband to take pictures of me. If he complains, I remind him that he's going to need a lot of really great shots to share with the crowd, and I want the kind that show me looking real, enjoying life with the people I love.

I don't want my funeral to be full of filtered, staged, glammed up, or photoshopped red-carpet pictures. At the end of the day, and the end of my life, none of this is going to be about looking pretty. No, I want the people who love me to remember the real me—the person who hugs everyone the first time I meet them, and laughs with my family, and loves Jesus with my whole heart, and smiles every chance I get, and gathers courage to walk through every door God opens. I want them to see a woman who was more than pretty. I want them to see a woman who lived out her God-granted destiny.

And I want the same for you. At the end of this book, I want you to know why you faced the challenges you did. I want you to know who you are—not just on the outside, but who you really are, what your strengths are, what your calling is, and what Jesus will see when He looks at you at the gates of heaven. I want you to feel passionate about the seeds you're planting. Will people remember your kindness? Will they remember that you lived with integrity? That you lived with a beauty that shone through in how you carried yourself, in how you spoke, in how you took chances? Will they remember that you were forgiving, because you were forgiven?

That's who you really are. The outside stuff of being pretty will all go away. But your soul, your character, your personality, your laughter, and your joy will stay. Those are the things people will celebrate when you're gone. That's what makes you fully you and fully loved.

So girl, put this book down and go out to own those things. Be all of yourself. Be all that God created you to be. You are amazing. You are unique. You are beautiful. And you have an incredible future in front of you. Thank you for letting me be a part of it.

As I say every day on the radio, I love you, and I mean it.

Acknowledgments

I'm so honored and excited to get this book done. It has been in my soul for a few years and to actually get it done and to work with amazing people is a blessing. Big thanks to my literary agent, Shane Norman; my book publishing team at Simon & Schuster including Beth Adams, Becky Nesbitt, Shida Carr, and Min Choi; my husband for his patience; and my executive assistant, Misty Anderson, for being a sounding board. To my publicist, Jojo Pada, my legal team at Fox Rothschild, and most important my family and friends that helped to shape my life's journey, thank you! This book did not happen by itself although it came from my heart. I was able to pour my heart out and have people work with me that understood what I wanted to say. I believe that it will be a blessing to many people not just to me.

While growth is beautiful, stretching is very painful and I've been stretched in so many ways in my life that it's made certain muscles strong. The muscle of knowing who I am is so strong only because it's been more than stretched and torn down. You'll read some of that in this book and hopefully it'll bless your life the way it's changed mine.